PEACE
PLEASE

Chris Lohden (signature)

BY THE GRACE OF GOD

A ROADIE'S TALE

Christopher M. Lohden

TO: John
Enjoy!!

These words are written for you to live the dream. If you had one chance to just try and make your dream come true, would you take it? I can promise you, if you take the leap, people will appear, hold your hand and show you the way! I have to thank J9 for holding my hand, walking with me and making me trust myself. I thank my whole family for letting me be me. I thank Amber for taking care of me when I should have been dead. I also thank every one of you that lived on the busses with me. I owe each and every one of you my life. Most of all I thank the Lord for carrying me on his back as I wandered through the maze of understanding.

WELCOME
THROUGH MY NIGHTMARE

Indianapolis, actually Deer Creek, to be exact, was the site of the infamous acid trip. (For years to come, the stagehands would just look at me and laugh when I walked in with other tours.) We loaded in. I did all of the trusses over the audience, as usual. It took most of the day, and then I sat stage left in the back hallway watching the dimmers. That was my job during the show. As you may know, the Grateful Dead would do two sets every show. Well, in between the sets, Chuck wandered by and handed me three hits of LSD. We had two shows there, and this was just the first show, so I figured it would be cool to take a hit as the band went on for the second set. I would have the show and the whole next day to chill for load-out. As fate would have it, by the end of the show I was not tripping. I was feeling absolutely no effects from the acid, so I took a second hit. I shut down the system for the night and hopped on the bus. It was really weird that I was so straight still. We got back to the hotel, and everyone decided to meet at the hotel bar for some drinks after cleaning up in our rooms.

I headed up to the room, took a shower, and still felt as normal as I could be, so I took the last hit of acid. OOOPS! As soon as it hit my tongue, the room shot about a hundred feet away, and I was standing in space looking in. Within seconds, I was so far out of reality that I just sat on my bed and watched all of the crazy things that were passing through my thoughts turn into vivid reality. I can't and probably never will remember all of the crazy things I saw that night. I remember at one point seeing red and blue flashing lights outside my window, which was about seven stories up. I guess the aliens came by for a visit, God only knows.

At ten a.m. my phone rang; it was my crew chief. He said that the fans had broken down the fence during the show last night at the back of the lawn in the venue and that we could not do the show that night. He said to get on the bus and we were going to load out and head to the next city. I

1

had come down a little, but not much, so I grabbed everything that I could, threw it in my suitcase, and headed down to the bus.

The walls were expanding and contracting the whole way to the elevator. When I got in the elevator, it closed in on me and there was just enough room for my suitcase and me. When the doors finally opened, the whole elevator car became huge. I didn't even check out at that point, I just headed to the bus. When I got to the bus, there was no one on it yet so I went straight to the back lounge, picked up a newspaper, and hid behind it. I would have read it if it hadn't looked like a page of paper painted with a flat grey paint.

A little while later, Chuck showed up on the bus, came into the back lounge, pulled down the paper that I was looking at, and asked what the hell I had done. I just peered up at him and said, "I ate the acid you gave me." His eyes got the size of grapefruits as he asked, "All of it?" I said yes. He then gravely asked me if I knew what that meant. I responded with, "I didn't know last night, but I'm pretty sure this morning." He shook his head as he told me that the three hits were "four-ways" (four hits each) and that they were just made the day before. He then decided to inform me that it was the freshest acid I would ever have and that the twelve hits that I had taken put me in the category of the acid tests back in the '60s. I informed him that it would have been nice to have that information last night when he gave me the LSD. He just smiled that evil smile of his and turned the paper over so that it was right side up, then told me not to tell anyone else what I had done. He said if it got real bad to find him and he would get me through the trip.

Everyone else got on the bus, and we headed to the gig. I just hid in the back behind the paper and stayed quiet the whole ride. When we got to Deer Creek, I headed down to the audience and got my stagehands. They all gathered around me and I said, "Guys, I'm a wreck, please do your best to take this rig down. If you have any questions, I will try to answer them, but I can't promise anything." My pupils must have been as big as my eyeballs. I couldn't even start to think with any kind of reality. To my surprise, my stagehands went straight to work and kicked ass all morning. I remember them fucking with me a bit, and laughing a lot, but they got everything down and put away perfectly. To this day, I still send out a "Thank You" every time I even get near Indianapolis.

I had to load a truck on that tour, and that turned into quite an adventure. My hands looked like bubbles, so you can imagine what the road cases looked like as they came into the truck. Anyway, somehow I made the square-ish boxes fit into the triangles, circles, and all kinds of gaps I saw in the truck. All I can say is thank you mom for buying me that little toy where you fit odd-shaped pieces of plastic into the holes on the octagonal-shaped ball when I was a toddler. The memory of that toy got me through the truck pack. I think the loaders wanted to kill me as I said things like, "that box spins and fits in that triangle," but I had a blast watching everything change shapes as they lifted it.

After all of the lighting was in the truck, I headed to the bus. I crawled straight in my bunk to watch the hallucination show that was to last for a few days. I wish I could remember all of the crazy things that I saw in there. I should have decided to write this book back then. I do remember lots of elephants marching in and out of my bunk. I spent the whole ride staying out of everyone's way on the bus. I would wander from the front lounge to the back lounge, drink a few beers, hop in my bunk, and watch whatever show my brain would cook up.

We all live differently from each other. Each one of us has our own experiences and grows in different directions, just to end up in the same place. We have experiences that shape us as humans and show us the directions to take. My story is hopefully different from yours, but in the end we all end up dead. The time we spend here is so precious, and we should all take a little time to look at what we have done.

AFTER THE BEGINNING

Mine begins with a loving family in suburban Tampa, way before it turned into the metropolis that it claims to be now. I grew up in a lovely house in a great neighborhood, but, being a boy, I found my way into trouble easily. My friends and I were always up to mischief and always trying to hide the things we did from our parents. From shooting out windows with BB guns to breaking into houses, we found trouble to be a way of life. We all rode motorcycles in the woods, fished in the canal behind the house, played football in each others yards, and enjoyed life the way all boys in the '70s did. As far back as I can remember, I wanted to be a rock star, and not just a rock star, a lead singer! At one point I stole all of the blue and red light bulbs from outside the house and made my room into my own rock star stage. Between the poster of Farrah Fawcett and the life-size poster of David Lee Roth I would Sing to the top of my lungs to "Toys in The Attic." I spent hours in my room alone, putting one album on after another while reading every word written on those album covers. At one point I found a way to place my pillows perfectly between the two mammoth speakers and hear the clearest, loudest music imaginable. The only thing I wanted to do was to listen to bad-ass rock and find some way to get to the next concert that was coming to Lakeland or St. Pete.

About this time, the dude from across the street was hanging out with his buddies in a tent that they would set up next to their house. It was a sleepover, and it was a thing that caught on with all of us kids before too long. The best part about the older guys starting it was that they found a way to buy beer. After about the third sleepover, Joe, the guy that lived across the street, would hide a few of the beers for us younger guys. He would give them to us the next day. They were hot and kind of gross, but that never stopped us. From the beer we were then introduced to vodka, which we were told could not be smelled on your breath, so we started to drink a lot of that. Before long, we were smoking pot. I don't think we ever found any speed or coke until we were all in high school. With the partying and the music, I just knew I was on my way!

My mom, on the other hand, had her own ideas. She wanted me to play sports, but there were some rules that went along with that. First of all, her boy was not going to get hurt playing football. Secondly, she was not going to sit through a boring baseball game every weekend. Those were the team sports in America at that time. When I was eight, she came home one day and said that we were going to go and join this team that played soccer. I asked her what it was, and she didn't really know, but she said that you only use your feet to kick a ball in a goal, no hands. Well, what could I do? At least it was a sport on a team, and boys need that.

As it turned out, we would spend most of the next fourteen years in the world of soccer. I played for school and clubs; it was my whole existence for most of the year. I would practice after school for the school team, then later in the evenings for the club teams. The whole world for me revolved around playing soccer. It really was a great time, and it kept me out of so much trouble that my friends in the neighborhood were stirring up. (Although I would still party every chance I had.)

When I finished high school, I ended up in Ft. Lauderdale, playing for Nova University. This was in the heyday of spring break. There are no words for the mayhem that took place in the '80s in that town. Most people had a week to go crazy down there, but for us, it was about two and a half months of fun. Every week, there would be a new set of colleges moving in for drinking, dancing, and wet t-shirt contests. For a kid at eighteen, that was a smashing good time. Rock and Roll touring was at its height, discos were still the rave, and the girls were drunk and out of control. All of my friends had long hair and trim, tan bodies from all of the soccer, so the mayhem for us just grew every week.

There were so many bars on the beach back then. You could start on the south end at the Elbow Room and work your way all the way up the beach to The Parrott. I think that those two bars are still there, but the rest, I am sure, have passed on. There were so many people walking up and down the street that the sidewalk could not hold the crowds. The police would have to block off traffic in one lane along the bar side of the street for the people walking. Back then it was a two-way street, two lanes traveling each direction, with slanted parking on the beach side. Now it is one way with a sidewalk where the parking used to be. Nothing in Florida stays the same, but I guess if you want to make it into a real state, you must conform to the whims of those from the north.

There are so many stories from that time that I could fill a book with just those. Some of the best times were spent walking up and down that strip, in and out of bars. We used to steal liquor out of the wells from Penrod's right off the street. For some reason, they would set up this huge bar on the patio that ran the length of the hotel, with the back of the bar facing the sidewalk. I'm not sure how many locals filled their apartments with liquor from that bar, but all of my friends did.

The best place to be around four o'clock p.m. was outside The Candy Store. There was this big platform set up right by the wall that surrounded the pool. The wet t-shirt contest was held on that platform every day. You could imagine the traffic on A1A at that corner. Every day it turned into a parking lot while the beautiful young ladies whipped off there wet tops for the whole block to cheer. The Button South, and Summer's with the pool in the back, had some pretty fun shows, but that was all inside and at night.

I guess when you grow up in a world like that, you keep looking for the next big step in that direction. Little did I know, that entire soccer world that I had grown up in was about to end, and the new exciting world of mayhem would begin. All of those parties, rock concerts, and all around foul behavior in that paradise called Ft. Lauderdale were coming to an end. The cops started arresting everyone, and the whole atmosphere of spring break was on the way out. I guess the city wanted to make the town a nice beach resort for the Europeans, like so many other beach towns in Florida evolve into. They did a great job, and now instead of the cheap hotels and cheap rates, there are beautiful resorts and high prices.

I only played a couple of years at Nova. It was a great time, until I quit trusting the coach, who had coached me in high school. That world was not what I had expected. The politics of soccer had gotten to me. I was tired of thinking that I was a good player. Yes, I was getting money to play, my school was paid for, and I was getting an education. But as has happened a lot in my life, I guess my temper (or lack of controlling it) started me on a different path. I got mad at the players that were getting ahead in the soccer world. I thought that I was better and that I was just getting taken advantage of because I was a friend of the coach. I think the coach needed to show the other players through advancement and recognition that they were important. I think maybe I was the one who the coach thought didn't need that sort of recognition. I don't think I needed it as much as the others, but it got old to me to sit and watch those politics.

I left Nova and moved back to Tampa. I went to school at USF and tried out for the team there. I made the team, but I found out shortly after that that the coach at Nova never released me. He had told me that he would and that there would not be any problems, but the politics of soccer kept revealing themselves; apparently, a friend and coach will lie and treat you with contempt for no real reason at all. As I have stumbled through my life, I have found that there are so many people like that it gets hard to keep track. Well, I had to red-shirt that year at USF, and found that I was either not as good as I thought I was or that no one really wanted me out there anyway. I never got a scholarship, never really felt any support on the field from anyone.

As time passed, and the money that I had saved was dwindling down (due to my love of beer), I found that all of the classes I was taking were quite boring. I really thought that I wanted to be a teacher, and maybe I should have stayed on that path, but of course, I didn't. My dad wanted me to take some business classes and help him with his water softening company, but that was not anything that I wanted to pursue. I guess you just see yourself as so much more when you are young. Those dreams that you are taught to dream seem to lure you away from all of the things that could make your life simpler. My dad had a good company. He did well for us. We always had what we needed, and mostly what we wanted. Sure, as I found out later in life, my mom had to struggle with many parts of the life she had with my father, but we were always a family, a unit; when push came to shove, we looked out for each other.

I had run out of money, and without a scholarship for school it was time to go find a job. I had never been that good at finding a job. When I was in eighth grade, a friend of my mom got me a job in a warehouse cleaning medical rental equipment. I don't remember how long I did that, maybe a year or two. I do remember at the end there was this French kid that was older than me that got me in a bunch of trouble there. I was humiliated, young, and busy with soccer anyway, so that ended. I worked for my dad for a few summers, but that was no fun, as almost anyone who has worked for his or her father can attest. When I was in Ft. Lauderdale, the coach's wife worked for Sea Quest, a diving equipment company that had a warehouse there. I got a job through the coach to fill orders, pack boxes, and ship stuff all over the southeast.

So my experience for looking for a job was and is quite bad. I seem to have always had someone either offer me a job or find one for me. This was going to be a new experience for me! I didn't have the slightest idea as to where to start. As I was about to find out, I didn't get to find out. The guys that I drank with at the time had called my house and wanted me to go out drinking with them. Well, as luck would have it, I had no money, and I told them that I was broke and needed to find a job the next day. To my surprise, Mark said, "Don't worry, I got your drinks tonight. Come into the Sun Dome with us tomorrow and I will get you some work there." Well, that was good enough for me. So off I went to some college bar to get drunk and worry about work another time.

That was the introduction to the circus that would become my life for twenty years. I walked into the arena, where I had seen so many concerts, to get a job. I met this guy, Jeff, who hired me, and told me to show up the next day at eight a.m. with a crescent wrench. He also said to just push boxes where I was told to push them, and if I was asked to do anything else just tell them that I was a pusher. I was there at eight a.m., wrench in my back pocket, nervous, but making four dollars an hour, for the whole day. I started pushing boxes in the building, and this roadie grabbed me and said, "Come on, you are running motors now." I said, "I'm just a pusher," and he said, "Not anymore, take this pickle and run this motor." So not only did I have a new job, I learned how to run motors on the first day and did exactly what my boss told me not to do. I looked up as I was running the chain through a motor, and from behind the big elephant door came Jeff. He looked straight at me and made this face, then he just shook his head. As time would have it, Jeff turned into a great friend, and we traveled to many place on this earth working together. By the way, that show was Tina Turner at the Sun Dome, Tampa, Florida, September, 1987. What a strange world I had just dropped into.

There were so many rock shows at that time. It is hard to imagine. The ticket prices were not out of control like they are now—and, of course, the wages were nothing like they are now. That four dollars an hour worked out to be OK. We would get paid for eight hours, even if we only worked for a couple. We also got paid for four hours that night to take the show out, even if we only worked a couple then. We also got t-shirts, and, at first, a keg of beer, although, being at a school, that would all change soon. There was some sort of insurance problem with being on the clock all day and yet not being at work, so the wages went up to seven dollars an hour and we got paid for fewer hours. It all worked out to be about the same amount of money. I'm not sure how many shows I did there before I decided that that was what I wanted to do for a living. What I knew about life at that point was that you got a degree from school and pursued your goals. Well, with all of the drinking, partying, rock shows, and work, I looked into the theater program at USF.

I had always just made the grade to play soccer, so I had no idea what it would be like to study something that I really enjoyed. It was a great experience, and I never struggled again to make the grade, which had been my experience with school since I was a child. I didn't ever like schoolwork until I found theater. I loved school, just not the work. All of a sudden I was making As and it felt as if I was not trying. I found that I could work and drink all night and still get to school and make great grades. This was definitely the life for me. I just knew it. As time passed, I found new friends, more venues to work at, different companies to work for, and shows to do at school. We all drank and partied, made money, and had a ball.

This was just about the time when my dad died. He had a sudden heart attack while he was in a mall. They said he just fell down and died. They tried to get him back, but there was no way. The whole situation was one of utter disbelief. I had stayed out all night and gotten home in the morning. I think it was a Sunday, no one was home, and it was pretty eerie in the house. Something just was not right. My mom was at a conference, and she would not be home until the afternoon, but my dad should have been there. My sister should have been around as well, but she wasn't. As soon as my mom got home, not much later, the phone rang. She picked up the phone and I just watched her as she turned a color of white that I had never seen. She put the phone down slowly and asked me in a very strange voice if I could drive her to St. Pete right then. I said yes and started to get things together. She just looked at me and said "I mean right at this moment."

I got my keys and we both walked to my car and got in. When we started to pull out, I asked her if she was OK. She said, "No, I think your father is dead." I asked, stupidly, "What do you mean?" She said we were going to the hospital and that we would know for sure when we got there. I started to ask but she cut me off and said, "They can't tell you that over the phone, you must be in person!" At that point, I just drove. We didn't say anything else to each other for the whole ride.

When we got to the hospital, I parked and we walked in. It was a small place. We were greeted at the door and they took my mom off to the side. When they were done talking, she came over to me and just said, "Yes, I was right." For some odd reason, I asked the person if I could see him, it just popped out of my mouth. She said yes and asked my mom if she wanted to go as well. She said no, so I went into this strange room with all of this medical equipment and saw what was left of my father. His body looked terrible. It was very bloated and purple all over. Of all of my worst nightmares, that may have been the scariest of them all, and it was real. I hugged his body and left the room.

To tell you the truth, I don't know when my mom got a hold of my sister, but she showed up right around that time. That would be the first time of many that we all just looked at each other with the thousand-mile stare, knowing that from that point on we were all we had. The three of us were the only people that would mean anything to each other, forever. It was an odd feeling, and it has never left. Even to this day, I can feel that same feeling when the three of us are alone together.

We went to church every Sunday, growing up. My dad taught a Bible study class and was pretty religious from what I knew as a kid. I had grown up in the church, and most of my friends were Christians. I have always considered myself a Christian, but I was a long way from understanding what that really meant. Once, my father had told me that he was here to accomplish a task. He said he was "told by God." I thought that was a bit strange, but my dad was a bit strange anyway.

He was Native American, and he was also a healer. He had a strange way of healing that he never really showed anyone. When I was a kid, I had warts all over my hands, thirteen to be exact. One day I was whining about them, and he came over to me and asked me if I wanted them to go away. I said yes. He said, "OK, I am going to touch each one and count them out loud. For the next week, try not to talk about them or think about them, and we will see what happens." Sure enough, the next week, they were all gone. I think that was the first time that I questioned my beliefs. That was not something that we learned in church; in fact, that was really weird. To this day, I wish he were alive so I could ask him about that.

Being a stagehand and then becoming a theater major had a few setbacks. There I was, not really a student, but a stagehand wanting a degree. I wanted to do well in school, which I did, but I wanted a Rock and Roll lifestyle. I was constantly getting pulled into teachers' offices to answer to why I would show up in the morning finishing my homework in the lobby, eyes red and reeking of alcohol. I didn't know at the time that just making the grade is not what they wanted for me. They wanted me to excel in the world of theater. I did try that for a while, and I think I was quite good at it. I designed shows at school and for several local companies. I enjoyed it immensely. I really liked when I designed lights for dance. Lights became the scenery, and the thought and work I put into those shows was very satisfying. I could not make any money doing the shows at school, so the circus of Rock and Roll filled all of my free time.

I was also doing a few shows for a theater company in Tampa. One of the shows was a Native American show. It was a one-man show by a guy named Homer, and it told the story of a man's grandfather, a shaman. I worked with that show for several years. We performed that show all over the country, as well as Scotland. Homer and I got to be pretty close friends over that time, and we had many discussions about Native American religion, as well as Christianity. Through these discussions, I began to really question the ways of Christianity. Throughout the next twenty years or so, I would spend loads of free time studying Native American ways. It seemed to be simple and true. Native Americans seemed to have the same ideas as Christiains yet the Christians didn't seem to live their lives by the things that they spoke about on Sundays. Native Americans walked the walk.

Studying in that way led me into a journey, a journey that would take twenty years to fully begin to understand. A journey that led me to question, as well as to finding answers to everything that I didn't understand. Taking that time in my life to study Native American ways was my path to become closer to my Lord, Jesus. By the Grace of God, I jumped out on a mission, a mission to live a life that not very many people get to live. I was sent out to experience all that the Lord had given to us, and find the answers, for myself, of who I am here to please. I had no idea that any of this was where I was headed. In fact, to my surprise, the Lord grabbed me and held me and walked me through the next twenty years.

Welcome to what I thought life was. Welcome, as well, to what I have found my life to BE!

LEAVING EVERYTHING BEHIND

There was this guy Marc, who had moved down from New York, that I started to work with often. Marc has been and I feel always will be one of those friends that you always search for through life. Marc worked at the famous Apollo Theatre before he moved down here. He had two children, and I am pretty sure that he didn't want them to grow up in New York City, the way that he had. This may not be the total reason for his move, but I'm sure it was part of it. Anyway, I would drive to Marc's house in the morning for coffee every day. Some days we would have a few cups then head off to a work call somewhere in town, other days we would just drink coffee all morning, get all jacked up, and smoke tons of cigarettes.

This became a daily occurrence during the week. Every day: wake up, head to Seminole Heights, drink coffee, talk, and smoke. We had so many conversations about so many things. I don't remember that many, but I did like to hear all of his stories from New York. He was quite a fixture up there. He had all of these biker guys that worked with him as stagehands. Marc had found a way to work with the union so everyone would get work, union and non-union together. The stories he tells are great fun. I remember when he spoke about living in a theater in the Village and working as a janitor. One day some girls were putting in a show and needed an electrician to hang some lights. Marc told me how he hung the lights, walked all over the grid above the stage with cables, and plugged them all in to dimmers for the girls.

Voila, STAGEHAND!

It is funny when you look back through time and see that almost everyone in this business started out doing some stupid job or floundering around through life and became a stagehand. The Lord definitely works in strange ways, and one of the strangest jokes he plays on humans is letting themselves find a way into show business. Talk about a way of life that is hard to explain. The only thing that I can think of doing is letting you in on what I have seen and done in the last twenty years. You can try and explain that life to yourself on your own terms.

Well, to get the ball rolling, I showed up, as usual, at Marc's house one morning, sat on the porch, and out comes Marc with a cup of coffee. He sits down and the first thing out of his mouth is, "You can't come over and hang out with me in the morning anymore."

I was thinking, "What the hell did I do?" That was what I normally thought when I was asked not to come around anymore. It had happened throughout my life, and, as I was to find, it would keep happening.

I asked why, and he said that I was going to have to pack my stuff and move to New York or LA, but that I could not stay in Tampa and work with him any longer. He said that I was pretty good at what I did and that I would waste myself on drugs and booze if I stayed here. He never told me, "You will never work in this town again," just that I would not work with him and hang out, wasting away on his porch.

As luck would have it, Marc knew people in New York and LA. I had come to trust him very much, and so when he offered to call for me, I took him up. Since I was doing so much rock and roll, I really thought that it would suit me best to go to LA and try to make it on the road. Marc called a guy named Drake, who told Marc to have me give him a call. I did, and he said that he could not send me on the road until I worked in the shop in LA first. He said that he had sent a few guys out lately, by word of mouth, and that they made a mess out on the road, so he had to cover his bases.

Within a week of Marc telling me that I had to go, I had all of my belongings in my Nissan Pulsar, along with my $1500 that I had saved up, and was waving goodbye to my mother on the driveway. When I look back now, I can only imagine how my mother felt that day. I still get a lump in my stomach when I think about it. Sure, I was worried what was out there, in LA, three thousand miles from all that I knew, but for her…I don't even think I could ever imagine.

I took a week to drive out to LA. I stopped in Vegas to visit with a friend of mine, Eric. We had a great time. Back then Vegas was still pretty small. We went rock climbing and even chased some wild horses in his jeep. It was a nice stop; I had been pretty worked up about this new life I was about to begin. It really took the edge off. I had a friend that was living in North Hollywood, Jay, and when I got to LA, he let me crash on his sofa for a few days while I got settled and found a place to live. I stayed there for a week or so, while I got into the shop at Light and Sound Design (LSD). Then I found a room in a house in Thousand Oaks.

At LSD, in the shop I got paid seven dollars an hour. I really had no idea how I was going to live on seven dollars an hour and figured I would stay until I ran out of money, then head home if I didn't get on the road. At least I had a plan. I think that was the last plan that I have ever had. As time would pass and work would come and go, the whole idea of a plan has never taken seed in my brain again.

Drake introduced me to this English guy, Joe, who in turn handed me off to Flee, who would be my boss on the shop floor. Flee was a pretty cool guy, he sent me up to a loft over cable-land to re-wire a bunch of three-cell cyc lights. So off to work I went. There was a stack of about thirty of these lights to wire, so I just put my head down and started wiring away. Well, at about six p.m., the lights started getting dark, and I headed down from my perch. Flee was standing at the bottom of the stairs with this strange look on his face. Seems he had forgotten all about me up there and said he was sorry, the workday ended at five; he would pay me for that hour anyway.

I was prepared the next day. I had a sandwich for lunch and everything. Back then, lunch was pretty fun. LSD made their own trusses, and had a welding shop in the warehouse. The welders were all these really big guys, and they would run their mouths all during lunchtime. They were funny as hell. All I remember was just sitting there laughing and keeping my own mouth shut. LSD sold the welding department over some insurance stuff, and all those guys went to work in a new place called Total Fabrications.

I met a guy named Randy while I was working on the cyc lights. I had seen him before as a stagehand in Florida, but didn't know him. We worked on the cyc lights and ended up talking most of the day. He had a show at the Ventura Theatre that weekend, and he got me on the call with him. We ended up working well together, so he asked that I do some more jobs with him. That was about two weeks into my shop life, and I thought, "Cool, this is going to work out."

It was better than working in Florida, where I was a stagehand and a rigger, because I was actually setting up and maintaining the lighting system. I used to just show up and build the shows and tear them down for one show. This was kind of cool. Randy took me along on a three-show run with the band Live. We did a show in LA, then a couple in San Diego. To make things easy, we stayed at his house in Compton between shows. This was 1994; needless to say, I was going to get my understanding of racial tensions of LA that evening.

We pulled off the freeway and into a neighborhood in our Ryder truck full of lighting gear. As we came to a corner, a group of guys came out to the truck and stopped us. I was freaking out a bit. Randy rolled down the window and talked to the guys. At one point, they asked who was the white guy in the truck and what was he doing here. Randy told them we were working together and I would be with him at his house for a few days. They seemed OK with that and we drove to his house. I was shitting a brick. I had no idea what that was all about, and I don't think I ever will. I have never been a racist, and really didn't understand racism much. I have a better picture of it now, but I still don't understand it.

We got to Randy's house; there was no bed for me, but there was a mattress. I crashed hard, but woke up to some loud pops. Yep, guns. Lots of them, and close. It was freezing cold in the house, and all I had was my jacket, so I hopped in the closet, put the mattress over me, and went back to sleep.

Randy had a great time trying to find me the next day. When he woke me up, he was like, "What's up, dude?" I said I was cold and they were shooting guns all night, so I crawled in there. Well, from that day on, I have had to live with Randy saying, "Chris was so scared he was hiding under a mattress in a closet all night." Well, I guess it could be worse. I never argued this point with him; it makes for a better story when he tells it that way anyhow.

I guess, in the end, I did a good job on the shows, because Randy went back to the shop and told someone that I was too good to be in the shop wiring lights. I think he told a salesman at LSD, because within the next week I was on my way to the circus. Drake pulled me in the office and told me that there was a spot on Bryan Adams that was leaving the next week, and he said I should do it. Randy was off to do AC/DC or something, and thanks to him I was going to do Bryan Adams. I try to thank Randy every time I see him; I'm sure he is tired of hearing it, but thanks, Randy!

So there I was in the shop prepping a tour. My crew chief was this tall country guy named Rat, who ended up teaching me more than I could have imagined. I remember in the shop putting all of the gear together, marking everything, and wondering how I was going to remember all of the stuff that I was going to have to do. I was twenty-seven at the time, but I felt like I was straight out of high school. It seems strange, but every time we start a new chapter in our lives, we seem to walk in as a kid all over again.

Leaving to go on tour, I had no idea what to expect. Living on a bus with ten other guys was a whole new concept that I had to get around. It was quite a shock to the system, but as you spend a little time out there you just learn how to fit in and respect other people's space. Respect turns into a whole lesson within itself really quickly.

TYPICAL DAY

The buses were, and are now, very classy. As you walk up the stairs on the bus, the front lounge opens up to you. Usually, there is a couch or two, a table with bench seats, a counter with a sink, and a toilet. As you pass through the front lounge, you enter the bunks, where we sleep. Nothing that fancy, up to twelve beds, three high, six on each side of the bus. Today, there are televisions with DVD players in most of the bunks, but that has just really come about in the last seven years or so. Just past the bunk area, there is another door, which leads to the back lounge, which seems to take on a new name on every tour. (My favorite will always be the "opium lounge.") This lounge is always a little different on every bus. There is always a couch of some sort, either along the back or down one side, and a bench-type seat and table on the other side; instead there might just be a couch that wraps around the whole lounge, with either open space or a table in the center. I have even seen a back lounge that was an office. Some of the stars have the back lounge as a bedroom; there are buses that are even mobile recording studios.

The back lounge is usually where the mayhem begins. At night it is usually the first place to fill up with bodies and beer and all sorts of party substances. I remember many nights sitting back there on the night train. Staying up all night and straight to work first thing in the morning—a typical pattern way back in the beginning.

Everything that you can imagine is on these buses: refrigerators; microwaves; top-of-the-line stereos with tape, CD, and DVD players; big TVs; ice coolers; and a whole lot of crazy guys riding around the country, working horrible hours, sleeping in little coffins, and setting up gear for a show that will entertain anywhere from five hundred to a hundred thousand people. On big tours there could be ten buses, on small ones usually around two to four.

The whole system is a well-oiled machine. The days and weeks go by faster than you could ever imagine. Everything happens the same way every day from one city/venue to the next. When you go to see a show, pretty much everything that you see in that venue has been brought in and set up that morning and afternoon. A typical day on a typical three-to-five semi tour starts around nine a.m., at least as far as the personnel setting up the gear. There are no wake-up calls, and there is no one to look out for you when it comes to being on time for work. So at nine a.m. you had better be ready to unload the gear that you are responsible for. If you want breakfast or coffee, get up earlier!

After the first trucks are unloaded, the rigging gear should all be in the building, and there will be a few local guys (riggers) up in the ceiling dropping ropes to pull up all of the chains that run through chain hoists. These chains are what hold up everything that you see in the building. Every day in every different venue, these chains have to be hung in direct proportion to the stage, so every day for a rigger is a new day. No ceilings are exactly the same, so each morning the riggers have to be on the money, or nothing will match up to the stage. Once the riggers have gotten their measurements right and a few chains in the air, then all of the other work begins. Typically, the lighting guys start bolting together trussing systems, from which all of the lights will be hung. While the truss is still on the ground, they run cable for all of the lighting fixtures. The sound guys at this point will begin to assemble their PA systems. After the lighting rig is assembled, checked, and flown out of the way, the carpenters come in and build whatever set needs to be assembled. Then the backline guys find their way to the stage to put together all of the instruments for the band. As the backline guys are getting set, the sound guys start setting all of the monitor equipment, microphones, monitor wedges, and cables. While this is occurring, there are usually a few lighting guys up in the trusses pointing all of the lights where they need to be for the show.

While all of this is going on in the actual arena, there are tons of things going on in the back hallways. Production offices, tour management office, accountant's office, dressing rooms, and hospitality rooms are all being set up as per the rider (the contract which lays out what the artist must have each day of the tour).

The production office must be assembled just as the sound or lighting gear. All of the items that you would need in a daily office are in road cases and set up each day of the tour. Printers, fax machines, phone systems, and, as of the last eight years or so, Internet systems are all part of the mobile offices. Everything that happens in each city goes through this office. All supplies that are needed, all decisions that need to be made, and pretty much every part of the show each day is routed at some point through this office. This is also the place where all of the advancing of future venues is taken care of, including ordering all of the local stagehands, setting call times, sorting through all of the catering needs, and generally making sure that all of the local needs for the production are taken care of in advance of their arrival.

Tour managers usually travel with and take care of the bands. They take care of all of the needs of the artists, from all of the travel to the hotels and the whims that each member, inherently, will need. If there is room for a tour management office in a building, then it is always best to give them their own separate room, as this will keep the needs of the artist and the needs of the production in their own separate worlds.

The dressing rooms, as you may know, are a whole separate entity. That part of the rider ends up being the most important part of the day. Everything from the amount of towels, to the color of the M&Ms becomes important. Every story that you have heard is probably true. People lose their jobs over some of the items in these rooms. This is not to say that all artists must have everything every day the same, but as we all know, an artist is not always the same as a regular Joe.

The bottom line is that each of us out here on the road is here to make a fan have a great evening. Everything comes down to the artist and his or her relationship to the fan. None of us would have a job if it were not for that relationship. We are all hired to work for that relationship, so everything that we do is with the artist and their fans in mind.

When all of this is set—usually around four p.m. or so—the band shows up for a sound check. This is the time that everything is set and worked out for each particular venue. No room sounds the same, and every detail in this regard needs to be worked out as best as possible. In the older days, you would find only the sound and lighting engineers around for this bit of tweaking. Most of the other roadies would be back in their bunks getting in a little nap before the show and the load-out. But as technology has progressed so has the amount of attention needed to maintain the systems that are on the road. Nowadays there is not much time for naps.

If there is an opening act, when they go on the crew actually in the building is quite minimal. Usually it consists of the production manager (who never seems to get a break), the stage manager, two sound engineers (monitors and front-of-house), and a lighting director. This is the one time that there usually is a break before the show. When the opening act is over, everyone takes his place, checks all the systems for any problems, and gets ready to do what we all came to do: entertain you. If something breaks, and we can get to it, we fix it, then and there. You came to see the whole show, not just the parts that work that day.

When you have completely enjoyed your evening, we all hit the stage and begin to take everything apart and pack it back in the trucks. Whether there are two trucks or twenty trucks, the process takes from two to four hours. Everything is like clockwork, everyone has their responsibilities and does their part in finishing up the day. You learn right away that nothing can be left behind and that every box must be accounted for before each truck door is closed. Leaving something behind could mean a long, slow, and frantic day in just a few hours. Although things do get left once in a while, hopefully someone in another department will find it. This does happen, and the consequences are not always the most desirable. You could end up sleeping with the item in your bunk, or worse yet, getting it returned to you the next day right at the time that you need it, with a little price tag.

These are just my experiences. Every one of us has our own view on all of this craziness, so the truth and the fallacies seem to mesh. I have had a pretty good memory most of my life (even with all of the partying that I chose to engage in). Life is just not what you expect after you take the first step onto a bus. Everything that you think it will be is not, and everything that you are used to disappears. Friends become real friends, and enemies become acquaintances. You learn to live with all kinds of people and all kinds of issues. You generally spend most of the time finding ways to fix things that just don't seem to want to work.

There are politics out here, as in any job, but as time passes you learn to live with them until you can move along. As the corporations began to take over the world, they started to stick their heads into the wild, wild, west world of touring. As that happened, the politics got a little more prevalent. There has always been a little niche that you have to fit into, and there have always been ways to sort your way through them. But today, if you find a home, I think it is worth grabbing and keeping.

IN THE BEGINNING

So, my first tour was about to begin: Bryan Adams. I remember sitting at the airport with the Icon tech, a younger guy in charge of an old moving light that was broken more often than working. I asked him how we would remember the way to load the truck and how we would remember everything that we were supposed to know and in general just drove him crazy with nervous questions. His answer to it all was "Rat will take care of it."

Of course, Rat took care of it. As I found on that short tour, the crew chief is responsible for the whole lighting rig and all of the personnel problems, as well as all of the politics. He turned into an awesome teacher for me. We flew to Philadelphia on May 11, 1994. The next day, we loaded all of that gear into The Spectrum. Wow, what an eye opener. As a kid you think about all of these amazing towns and amazing teams that play in amazing arenas, and then you get there to find out that the buildings are old, the unions are tired and somewhat mean, and the world of Rock and Roll is not that glamorous.

When you load into the Spectrum, one truck pulls down the ramp, about thirty feet from the back of the stage. There is a group of non-union men that unload your truck. They get the gear off the truck and down the ramp, at which point they push the gear across a "no-man's land," where no one is allowed to walk or push boxes, to a waiting IATSE union crew who deals with all of the gear from that point on. There is literally a door that is about fifteen feet wide and fifteen feet high, just upstage of the stage, that everything has to go through in order to be used in the arena.

Everything that comes off the truck is in a road case: a hard case that protects the gear while it travels from venue to venue, city to city, truck to stage, etc. When you pull the gear out of those boxes, you then must find a place to store the empty boxes until that night when you will fill them back up and put them in the truck. There is no place to store boxes in the hallways behind the seating at the Spectrum, because there is no level ground; as you turn either way toward the arena floor down the backstage hallways, the ground of the hallway rises. There is a small area down the stage right hall off to the left to store boxes, and that is about it.

On the way out of the building, that night, it is all in reverse, including the union-to-non-union hand-off across "no-man's land," at which point the night becomes quite interesting. You can only imagine what the day ends up being when you have a tour with ten trucks or so. We had three and it seemed bad to me at the time.

We loaded all of the gear in on Thursday, the twelfth, and programmed the show that night. We did a show on Friday the thirteenth and loaded out that evening. That is where I got the answer to "How do we know how the gear goes back in the truck?" Rat had a list, and every box was accounted for going back in the lighting truck. Except one small box. As there were only a few places for storage, we were sent off to search for that box. It was nowhere to be found. Well, we were not leaving until we found it, I was told. Right before we finished loading the last truck, our dimmer guy found the box way out near front of house under some seats in the arena. That was my introduction to the world of a crew chief's responsibilities on the road. Everything was his, and he had to keep track of everything!

Four hours after the show, we hopped on a bus, and at eight a.m. the next day we loaded into Boston Garden. Having never slept on a bus before, I didn't sleep a wink. I just lay in my coffin all night, wishing to God that I could sleep. I came out of the bus in Boston to look at the bottom of some bridge and a truck backing up a huge ramp that went up two stories, to a door that had about two feet of clearance on each side of the truck. As everyone else got up and I began to follow them into work, I was thinking, "What in the hell have I gotten myself into?"

Well, at the old Boston Garden there was no loading dock, but rather, on the opposite side of the building, through the very old lobby and into a room next door to the front doors, sat two of the three trucks that we had on the tour. Every bit of gear had to get pushed off the trucks, through the lobby, and across the arena floor to the other end of the building, just to begin the day. Hanging the chain motors in that building was a rigger's nightmare as well. There were only three real beams in the ceiling. They were about twenty feet apart and ran from stage right to stage left. The riggers had their day cut out for them. The local riggers are really good there, and it took a lot less time than I thought it would. We put the show up, did the show that night, and four hours later got on the bus and headed for Buffalo and The Memorial Auditorium.

What can you say about the Memorial Auditorium in Buffalo? Well, as with Boston Garden, there was an historical ambiance here. It was an old building with an arena floor upstairs as well, and a loading dock which was a slab of concrete right on the lake. The gear came off the truck, through a small door, then got pushed up a catacomb of hallways that switched back and forth up to the arena floor level by forklifts. Once you got all of the gear through the almost impossible hallways, the arena was not that bad. It was big and had loads of storage behind the seats in the back halls of the arena.

All I can say is that I am glad that my first trip to that old building was not in the winter. I did make it there in the winter to experience the wind off the lake straight into the tunnels of doom, but that was later on. We did the Bryan Adams show, and just like the last three nights were on the bus in four hours heading to two days off in New Jersey.

That was the first night that I slept on the bus, and did I ever sleep! I went down hard. I'm not sure if the anxiety of a first run of shows finally let loose or if I finally just got so tired that I was beat. I don't know what time we showed up at the Meadowlands Sheraton, but I woke up at two in the afternoon in a huge parking lot, not actually knowing where to go or what to do. I looked in the "book of lies," grabbed my bag, and dragged it through the parking lot trying to figure out what building was the Sheraton. I checked in and passed out in my bed for another few hours. I don't remember ever being that tired. As time on the road passed, and I told other roadies of my first run on tour, I got the lowdown on those three buildings that I started in. Apparently, The Spectrum, Boston Garden, and the Memorial Auditorium were the hardest three arenas in the East. And as you can see now, The Garden, the Auditorium, and the Spectrum are all gone.

We loaded into the Brendan Byrne Arena, now the Izod Center, and I saw for the first time what a real arena load-in was like. It was not so bad actually. The day went very smoothly. The stagehands at that arena were great, and as I passed through there many more times I found that they were always great. There was a loading dock inside the arena; the truck beds sat flush with the arena floor, so we unloaded the trucks straight onto the stage. What a nice surprise after the fiascos of just a few days before. We did one show there and headed to Pittsburgh, where I was born, for a day off.

That would be the last time that I saw my grandfather in pretty good shape. He came to pick me up at the Westin William Penn, and I drove back to Glassport to spend the day with my mom's family. After he picked me up and asked me to drive, I saw that he was not the grandfather that I had remembered. You have to know that he was a proud old steel worker; he had built several of the buildings in downtown Pittsburgh. He operated many cranes and other massive pieces of machinery. He and my family lived through the whole decline of the steel industry. Pittsburgh is built from a proud group of men that built and made the parts for the infrastructure of our nation. When that industry vanished, so did the hearts and dreams of so many. To see the city now, with the clean air and beautiful rivers, is a sight to behold. Especially after going to visit my grandparents as a kid and seeing all of the smoke in the air and rivers full of coal barges. We had a great afternoon; I saw my grandmother and my cousins. I found that I would get to see and talk with many people that I would not normally get to visit with this new job. It seemed as though I would be in heaven, traveling around the world with bands. But as time passed by, I began to see that not only do you get to jump in and out of people's lives, you miss big changes, which pass you by why you're out somewhere else.

My grandparents moved down to Florida with my mom very soon after that. My grandmother could not take care of her husband anymore. She needed help, and as always my mom took them in, as she did with every wayward soul. I missed all of that. I was on the road, so I could not help moving them down from Pittsburgh. Sometimes I think of that time and think that I should have been around.

I got back to the hotel and crashed. The next day we loaded into the Civic Arena. Well, being from Pittsburgh, I knew that the roof opened, but I didn't realize that the ceiling was completely smooth. No beams or steel anywhere to hang chains. As I contemplated this for a moment, I noticed all these wire ropes hanging from the ceiling. They were all over the place. The riggers got to work on giant cherry-pickers, choosing and hanging each of our chain motors from the steel that was already attached to the ceiling. What a job, if you think about it: if you choose one wrong steel point from the ceiling, you may have to drop everything and redo all of the work that you have already done. Luckily, that was not the case, and although it took a long time to hang everything, the day went by, the show took place, and we were on the way to Cleveland that night. We played the Richfield Coliseum, and other than it being an old arena it was fine. From there we drove to Detroit for my first show at the Palace of Auburn Hills.

The Palace at Auburn Hills was a newer arena, and it has a great crew. There is a huge loading dock behind the stage, with tons of room everywhere. The steel above the stage is on chain hoists, so no one has to climb around in the steel to hang points. The steel comes to the stage, and you do all of the work from the stage itself. That was awesome to see and made the day go much faster than I had seen so far. All in all, that was the best day that I had up to that point. I was beginning to see a light at the end of the tunnel of this job that I had chosen. I'm sure that there were many more arenas like Philly, Boston, and Buffalo when the generation before me was doing this, but the way things were headed now seemed OK to me.

We drove to Minneapolis that night and had a day off at the Luxeford Suites. I had never been to Minneapolis, and I strolled around all day. It is a beautiful city. I remember it being very clean. I still get the same feeling when I am there even today. We played the Target Center in downtown Minneapolis the next night. This is another neat, huge building. The trucks pull into the venue and drive right though the building so that the tail of the truck is right next to the door where the stage entrance is. You dump the gear off of the trucks, and the truck drives right out the other side. I was not sure exactly why they did this until I returned a few years later in the middle of winter! The day was easy. The stagehands were really great, and to this day I still have phone numbers of some of that crew in my phone. I would never think of driving through that town without touching base with them. Minneapolis I have found to be a great city with so many wonderful people.

We left Minneapolis that night to arrive at the Rosemont Horizon in Chicago. That was the day that I really learned what it was like to work for a strict union. We literally could not touch any of our own gear. We were there to instruct and that was it. I am sure glad that we didn't start the tour there; by that point I had built my part of the lighting rig eight times, so I knew enough to explain it without doing it myself. It was a bit rough on the brain, but in the end you find that the reasons behind the union doing the things their way is actually good. You spend a lot less time doing physical work, and your back is a lot less tired at the end of the day. If you do forget that you are in Chicago, and you pick up a light and hang it, you will never forget again. They are very good at explaining that that is their responsibility and not yours.

We left Chicago that night and headed for Kansas City. We arrived at the Westin Crown Center Hotel. I crashed most of the day, and had some barbeque that night. The next day we headed to the venue, which was the Sandstone Amphitheater. Being from Florida, I had never seen an amphitheater. They just did not exist. In the northern states amphitheaters are everywhere, and as I was to find out in just a month or two, it was a big summer thing to get outside at night to see a show. They have built a few amphitheatres amphitheaters in Florida now, but as you can imagine, the nights are nothing like summer nights up north. We call the amphitheaters "sheds" on the road. The trucks just back up to the back of the stage, and the gear rolls right on to the floor. I can't tell you how fast that day went. As time passed, everyone that I worked with loved doing shed tours. We all looked forward to them. They are made for a show to go in and out quickly.

From there we headed to St. Louis, to the Riverport Amphitheatre. Two sheds in a row, I was so happy. The Riverport amphitheatre Amphitheater and the town of St. Louis would end up being the scenes of some amazing stories, as time passed by on the road. This trip, as you can tell, was all about work and me learning the ropes. I will get to the amazing stories soon enough, but for now, all I can say was that I was really enjoying learning about sheds.

That night we headed to Nashville and played the Municipal Auditorium. It is an older building, but the day went fine. There is a loading dock and the crew, as you can imagine, is pretty good. We stayed in Nashville that night, and were scheduled to fly to San Jose the next day.

None of us had heard of Southwest Airlines at this point. It was a regional airline out of Texas that was growing quickly and had a good reputation. The only problem at that point, or at least that day, was that they had no flights from Nashville all the way to San Jose, or even San Francisco. (I'm not sure where we flew into at the end.) We all know Southwest Airlines now, and I enjoy flying with them, but we didn't have any idea what it was all about that day. As is the case now, they do not serve food. They do, however, serve peanuts and sodas. We stopped, like a city bus, four or five times all the way across the country. None of us ate anything but peanuts that day, as there was never enough time to get off of the plane and grab food.

The last stop before San Jose was LA. Half of the crew just got off of the plane. I was pretty new, so I figured that I should just stay put. They rented a car and drove the rest of the way. The next show was not for two days, so in hindsight I should have done the same. Anyway, we arrived in San Jose around twelve hours after taking off in Nashville. Each one of us ran to the nearest food stand in the terminal! We also stopped at In–N-Out Burger on the way to the hotel. We stayed at the Beverly Heritage Hotel in San Jose, and to tell you the truth I don't have any idea what I did on that day off. We played the San Jose Arena, which is a lovely newer arena, where I met several stagehands that I would grow to know well over the next twenty years. We did that show and headed to LA.

As is the case in LA, you see things on TV and they look huge, then you get there and it is quite quaint. This is the case with the Greek Theatre just up the hill from Los Feliz. You unload trucks on these very small loading docks right next to the stage. The stage is quite small, and the seating itself wraps around the stage. I would have to say that it is a great place to see a show, but there are several things to overcome while working. You have to adjust for the low ceilings, the stage is small, and there is not any room to store things, so they go down an elevator into the unknown. The best part about the day is that you are working with the union, Local 33; just behind New York's Local 1 sits 33. They are awesome at what they do. They have seen show after show and have a solution for every problem. You basically just tell them what you need and it is done. We did two shows there and stayed at the Sofitel Ma Maison right across the street from the Beverly Center.

I had kind of got the hang of this roadie stuff by now and was out at Barney's Beanery for a few beers. This is when it still had a bar to the right side and a restaurant to the left as you looked at it from the street. You could still smoke in the bar side then, as well. I ran into a few backline guys from the tour, and one of them had a great room on the top floor of the hotel. We went back there and opened the automatic window and looked out over the lights of LA as we emptied his minibar. That was the first of many mini-bar nights. We went back to the Greek Theatre the next day and did the show, loaded out, and headed to Phoenix for a show the next night.

We played the America West Arena, which is purple. I really remember that. The building is great, loading dock inside just down the hall from the arena, and the crew has always been good as well. We did the show that night and headed to the Phoenix Hilton Suites. That was the last show of the tour for me. I had a few drinks with the guys and went to bed. We all flew back home the next day, and when I arrived I realized that three and half weeks had passed. To me it felt like a week as much as it felt like a year. That was my first tour beginning to end: May 11-June 5, 1994. The rest of the main crew went to Germany at the end of the month, but I was headed to a very interesting tour, to say the least. This is the beginning of the real circus. I was in no way prepared for what I was about to get myself into.

THE GRATEFUL DEAD

Even the beginning of this one is a bit of a haze, as you could imagine. I am really trying to remember the beginning. I know I was in the shop, meeting everyone and putting it all in a truck. From there, the schedule says we went to Sacramento, and I remember being at Cal Expo, but I mostly remember the loading in and programming days in Las Vegas at the Silver Bowl. That is where it all came together as to what a party really was. After a grueling load-in, in 115-degree weather, I found that the cocaine was going to start flowing and wouldn't stop for a very long time. The amounts of that drug that were consumed over the next several years would be legendary. I was no stranger to the drug, but I was in no way a seasoned veteran like most of my new friends. I began to find my way through the world of coke and learn the ways of the veteran. What a trip that turned out to be! No pun intended there.

Out of the hotel and into our two minivans, we left the hotel for the Silver Bowl to load in the entire show. This was in 1994, remember. We made a turn off of the strip and headed up Tropicana Blvd. Before long we passed the Liberace Museum and were in the middle of the dessert. It was about a twenty-minute drive of absolutely nothing before we pulled up to this stadium in the middle of nowhere. As the new guy I wasn't ever allowed to go on the stage, so I put up all of the lighting equipment that surrounded the stage. There were several trusses in the pit, in front of the PA on each side, and these things called Dead Sheds on the field in the middle of the crowd. To this day, I am amazed that they never got disrupted by any fans on those fields; miraculously they just left them alone.

It was 115 degrees on the field. At one point, it measured 136 degrees at front of house in the shade. My stagehands and I would work for about fifteen minutes then sit under the stage for fifteen minutes and drink water. It was miserable! There was a point where the Vari-Lite console had to have dry ice inside of it just to work. The day went on for what seemed like forever.

When we were finally up and running and the stagehands had all gone home for the day, I got a call on my radio calling me to the dimmer pit. That is where all of the dimmers and power distribution go for all of the lights that we ran during the show. To my surprise, after all that work and sweat, there was a drawer pulled out with a huge pile of cocaine. I walked over and was told grab a line, good job today. So there I was, not the first time and not even close to the last, bent over a dimmer drawer snorting up the huge line laid out for me. Before long I was as high as I could be; it felt awesome. I wandered off and climbed to the top of the scaffolding so that I could see the lights of the Vegas strip in the distance. What a sight to behold. There I was, high as a kite, looking across the dessert and working for the biggest touring act in the world. I was on cloud nine. I came back down after a while and sat in that desert summer night with the rest of the guys on the crew and talked and did lines way into the night as the LD and programmers programmed until morning. When the sun rose, we turned everything off and went back to the hotel. When I finally fell asleep, I slept right up until the time we were to leave to go back.

The cocaine just kept flowing while we were in Las Vegas. We did three shows there, and the whole time I was there I was either recovering in my hotel room at the Alexis Park Resort or sitting on the side of the stage in our dimmer area watching the show. There was a point during the show where one of the Deadheads had eaten a little too much acid and climbed over the barricade, with no clothes, and proceeded to run around the side of the stage before he was caught. They took him to the EMS guys, who apparently treated him. I didn't think anyone could make it onto the "sacred stage." That was one of the biggest rules of the Dead. No one was allowed on stage until the stage manager approved him.

I guess I should explain some of the rules that were all around that tour. Being the size that it was, and the amount of time that the Grateful

Dead had spent touring, there were many rules. There was a lot of secrecy in the rankings of this tour. There was a hierarchy that let you know what boundaries you were allowed too cross.

The rules were laid out were according to what department you were a part of. The backline guys were in charge of everything. They made the rules. The sound company and the employees of Ultra Sound were the next in line. Ultra Sound had been doing sound for the Dead forever, and they were very important in the eyes of the backline. The caterers were somewhere in the realm of the sound guys. The Dead carried their own cooks and catering everywhere they went. There was a stage catering workbox upstage center that was completely full of every snack that you could think of, from bags of gummy bears and every candy bar ever made to a full espresso setup. There was Kona coffee brewing at every hour of the day. This box was only available to the backline, sound company, and the stage manager. There was a roadie that manned this box, kept it stocked, and delivered anything that those guys wanted whenever they wanted it.

The next in line, as far as importance, were the lighting guys, and we were not very important. For example, if we had a broken light in a truss over the stage, we would have to inform our crew chief, Frank, who would then call the stage manager, who would then talk to Steve, who answered for most of the backline requests and who would make a decision as to whether or not we could climb up to the light and swap it out. After that decision was made, then the message would go all the way back down the chain before we could put harnesses on and find a rigger to watch us as we went and swapped out the light. I know it sounds like a big fiasco just to fix a light, but as I found out, it worked out great for us that had to do the work. It would usually take about half an hour to get the answer, so if you were just snorting a big huge line of coke when the first step of calls came down the radio, you knew that you could stop and be in good shape to climb by the time you got an answer.

The last in the line were the video guys. They were not far behind us lighting guys, but at least we weren't last.

As I said, there was a catering crew that traveled with us and cooked all of our meals. The food was great. They would get in early in the morning and start cooking breakfast. The lighting and video crew went to work right away, so we usually didn't have time for breakfast. That was fine, because we had tons of food on the bus. When it came time for lunch, we always looked forward to some of the best and healthiest cooking on the planet. We did have a few lighting guys that only ate hamburgers, and they were always taken care of, but I loved the food and would pass on the hamburgers every time. Dinner was like a feast every night. The best part about the catering came at the end of the night during a multi-night stand in a single city. As we left the building to go back to our hotel, there would be bags at the back door with our names on them. Each bag had a small meal in it, usually a sandwich, some chips, a piece of fruit, and a drink. One thing that was never looked past on that tour was the food. That type of caring even showed up on the bus.

Each crew had their own bus and had to take care of all of the issues that would arise on their own. Production basically just handed each crew a bus and that was that. Frank took it over from there and made all of the bus calls. If we broke down, it would be Frank's responsibility to take care of it and get us to work on time.

There was this other cool responsibility that Frank had on the bus, and it was stocking it with supplies. I had never what I saw on that tour, and I am sure I will never see it again. As I said, the food was always amazing, and that spilled right over to the generosity of the bus stock. The first day that I was on the bus, Hodgie was walking around with an 8x11 note pad asking everyone what we wanted on the bus. He would hand them the pad, and when they were done he would rip off the page and pass it to the next guy. He came to me and handed me the pad. I put down a few things—peanut butter, jelly, bread, ham, cheese, mustard, and beer. It was not so much to ask for. I gave Frank the pad, and he shoved it back at me and said, "Fill the page." I told him I really didn't need much more, and he just told me to fill the page, and talk to the rest of the crew before I ordered cigarettes!

It took me awhile, and after talking with the other guys, I filled out most of the page. The thing about the cigarettes was that we would only get a carton of each brand of smokes, so everyone that smoked had to order a different brand or you would have to split the carton with someone else. That would never work. I liked Marlboro Lights, but those were taken, so I started smoking Merit. The guys would trade now and again, but I got used to them.

So now Frank had compiled this huge list of bus stock and tuned it in. To my amazement, when we left the first city, there were about ten shopping bags on the front lounge sofa. Everything that was on that list, from Pop-Tarts to rolling papers filled, the bags. We all stocked the cabinets and went about our business. What I came to find out as we were leaving the next city was that the whole list got delivered again. It was the weirdest thing in the world to me. There was so much food on the bus by the end of the tour. I began to realize why everyone had two suitcases; at the end of each run we split up everything and took it home for the house.

From Vegas we headed to San Francisco and played the Shoreline Amphitheatre. We loaded in there and stayed all night to program—or party, as it would turn out to be. Being that it was San Francisco, the home of the Dead, you could imagine the amount of drugs that were consumed. We had set up our dimming area, off stage left, under the raised platform used for viewing the show. There was a set of stairs to get up there, so we made a whole labyrinth of boxes to keep that separate from our dimmer area. For three days we smoked pot, snorted coke, and dropped a little acid back in that cave of boxes. That was the first of many sightings of Bill Walton, the basketball player. He was a huge Deadhead and showed up at many of the shows that I did.

We stayed at the Embassy Suites in Mountain View, and whenever we were near the hotel you could find us at the fireside lounge in the Peppermill. I'm not sure if we made it through all of the drinks with umbrellas, but we sure tried. From there we headed back across the country to Vermont and played the Franklin County Field. We played one show there and headed to JFK Stadium in DC. That was the best place as far as hotels. We stayed at the Watergate, and I'm sure that I am not the only person with a Watergate hotel robe in my closet. After DC we headed for Indianapolis, to play Deer Creek Music Center. In the future, that would be the site of the never-ending trip I described before, but as we went through this time there was only lots of cocaine and pot for our pleasure. From there we went to Chicago and played Soldier Field, and then finally a day off in St. Louis. I had been to St. Louis one time in the late '80s, to do the play that I used to travel around with, *A Shaman's Dream*, but I had no idea that this was one town that would live with me the rest of my life.

After sleeping in a bit at the hotel, Jay and I headed to the mall, which is the old train station, in downtown St. Louis. We were shopping and, quite frankly, getting a bit bored. We were thinking about going to a brewpub for some beers and calling it a night, when all of a sudden Roy shows up at the exit to the mall and asks us what we are doing. We told him, and he counters with, "I know this place, it is like a twenty-dollar cab ride, but the chicks are amazing, and I got laid out of there." Well, splitting twenty dollars for a cab didn't seem so bad, and we really didn't have anything else to do, so we went back to the hotel, got sorted, and called a cab. I know, you never get laid at a strip club! We all knew that, but Roy would not shut up about it.

Well, the place was across the river in East Brooklyn, and before you get there you have to cross the river. Makes sense, but one reason the cab fare is twenty dollars is because you have to go over this privately owned bridge, which has holes in it, and pay a toll (and hope to God that the bridge does not fall down). After the bridge straight out of *Escape from New York*, you drive through this wooded area that is just creepy, no lights anywhere, as scary as can be. After ten minutes of this, you come across a small town that only has strip joints from one end of the street to the other. It is like driving into Stripville. I don't think I have ever been to such a strange little town in my life.

We pulled up to this place called Roxy's. Roy said, "We're here," and in we went. We paid the cover and sat down at the bar for a drink, just looking the place over and enjoying the music. They played rock music, good late '80s early '90s rock! That was enough to want to stay for a while anyway. For some reason that music is just made for women to dance to—or better yet, swing around a pole. The place has three raised dance stages: one is in the middle of the place with chairs all around it, one is a small circular stage, and then there is a medium-sized stage in the back corner. There are mirrors on all of the walls and tons of black lights everywhere. As we finished our first beers, watching, just as Roy promised, the hot chicks, we decided to head to the back corner stage.

We watched a few beautiful girls dance on the stage and tipped them as they left. Jay, for some reason I will never know, watched all of the dancers through the mirrors. I never figured it out, but he said he had his reasons.

Anyway, this girl climbed up the stairs to dance, and no one could take his eyes off her. She had really short dark hair, this hot petite body, just rock hard, and started dancing to some really heavy metal-type music. I wish

I could remember the name of the song. She started dancing around the stage like a mad woman, she was unbelievable, and every guy at the stage was just mesmerized and could not take their eyes off her. At one point she jumped up in the air and landed in a split and just kept right on going. It was one of those sexually charged moments where brutality and sex walk hand in hand. She danced for three songs like that, and not a single one of us guys could pick our jaws up from the floor from start to finish. When she finished, breathing heavily and covered in sweat, she did her rounds to get her tips. I was sitting next to the stairs where she came down from the stage and was the last in line for the tips. She bent down and got right in my face and, as nasty as she danced, demanded that I give her a tip. Well I had a pocket full of "Jerry" money and would have given her the whole pile. I asked her how much she wanted. She just demanded a tip again, so I asked again, fully aware that in my sexually charged state I would give her what ever she wanted. She reached down, grabbed me by the hair, and demanded one more time that I give her a tip. Of course, the jackass that I am, I asked one more time, and to my surprise, she leaned down and said a dollar would do. I pulled out the wad of money and gave her a dollar. She took it and came down the stairs. When she got to the bottom, she leaned over again and said, "Meet me at that bar in thirty minutes," and strutted right on into the back room.

Well, Jay and Roy came over and asked me what was going on and I told them. They said I was lying, and to be honest I was not sure what was true at that moment either. But I did keep an eye on my watch. We all wandered over to another stage and watched a few hot girls swing around the poles, but I couldn't enjoy any of it. I just kept thinking about getting my hair ripped back and being told to give her a tip. About twenty minutes went by, and I got up and headed over to the bar, really thinking that nothing was coming from all of this. I figure she saw the money I had and wanted to BS me out of some of it, buy her some drinks and whatnot. Well, she came right out of the back room and sat next to me at the bar. She asked if I wanted a shot, and I said yes. I went to pull out some money, and she told me to put it away. The shot came over, I had no idea what it was, and we touched glasses and threw them back. I asked her why she wanted to buy me a shot, and she said no one had ever fucked with her when she demanded a tip like that, and she liked it. And so the conversation dragged on for a while, into a bit of silence. She asked if I wanted another shot, and I did, we did, and as soon as I got it down my gullet she said, "I have not been with a man in five years, and I want to fuck you." I asked when and where. Without blinking an eye she said, "My place. I will meet you outside in thirty minutes." I said OK, and she headed for the back again. At that point I ordered a shot, slammed it down, and started to wonder what the hell was going on. I got another beer and tried to watch the other dancers, but that was getting nowhere in my mind. I wandered around the club for a while, just watching and drinking. I had no idea where Roy and Jay were, so I decided to find them. I found Jay at the back stage looking in the mirror, and I sat next to him and told him what was going on. He just laughed and said I made it up. I found Roy on the other side of the bar with this huge-breasted beautiful girl on his lap and told him I had a ride was leaving. He asked what was going on, but I just told him not to worry and or wait for me.

I started to go out the front door of Roxy's, and this bouncer told me if I left I would have to pay to get back in. At that point I figured if she didn't show up I would just cab it back to the hotel. I was pretty drunk at that point and had to work the next morning, so I figured that either way I was good. Sure enough, though, she pulled up and I got in.

We started heading down the scary wooded area. She told me that out there in the middle of nowhere you had to drive the speed limit, which was around 35 mph, because it was all speed traps and they pulled you over trying to get DUIs. She knew another way back to the city, so we didn't go over the *Escape from New York* bridge. We got to the city, and she pulled the car up to a curb behind this Italian restaurant. We got out and headed to the kitchen. At this point I was getting a little weirded out, but the suspense and the beers made it OK. We headed through the kitchen and up these stairs and ended up in her apartment above the restaurant. She opened the door, and this huge dog came running over and got all over me. She grabbed him by the collar and put a leash on him, then she told me to take it for a walk while she took a shower. At this point I was game for just about anything, so I just headed out the door and down the stairs. The dog took me down the street to a park in the middle of the city. We walked around and I held the leash while he pooped and pissed several times. After a while we were just kind of hanging out and his master came walking up.

She grabbed me and stuck her tongue in my mouth. What an amazing kiss. I have no words for that moment, actually. She shoved her hand down my pants and I was standing there, in the middle of a park in St. Louis, making out with this girl, hand in my pants and a dog on a leash. I quietly backed up and suggested we do this inside. She just turned and said follow me.

We ended up back in her apartment. She locked the dog in her room and we proceeded to rip each other's clothes off. Kitchen, living room, table, sofa, all were the scenes of this encounter. At one point we were in a doorway wrapped in an unimaginable position with the whole CD rack, and I mean hundreds of CDs, all around us, scattered throughout the room, and the phone rang. She moved away and answered it. She held her finger to her lips, instructing me to be quiet. I shut up as she yelled at the person on the phone—in what I am sure was a lover's quarrel. She slammed down the phone and said, "Get your clothes on now, I have to drive you to your hotel and get back home in one hour."

So I threw on my clothes and we ran down the stairs, out the door, and into her car. As she sped away from downtown St. Louis toward my hotel, she picked up this huge cell phone, called her girlfriend, and proceeded to start yelling again. As she got deep into the yelling match, she grabbed me by the hair, pulled up her skirt, and jammed my head right between her legs. So off to work I went. She got off the phone as we finally reached the hotel. As I got out of the car, she handed me a piece of paper with her phone number on it and said, "Call me." I asked her if she wanted tickets, and she said probably not, but call, then she sped away. So there I was, not knowing what to think, in front of the lobby of the Embassy Suites, my clothes half on and a huge smile on my face. I went into the hotel, headed to my room, and passed out.

The next day, we loaded the show into Riverport Amphitheatre, the day went along nice and smooth, and when I was finally done, I went to a phone and called. We spoke for about ten minutes, mostly of nothing in particular. Toward the end of the conversation I asked her if she wanted to come to the show. She said no, but I should call her when I'm back in town. And that was the end of that. I called her a few times in the upcoming months but always got an answering machine. I never got a page back from her, so I guess she worked everything out with her girlfriend. I'm just glad I was the right guy at the right time at the end of a five-year drought.

43

We did two shows in St. Louis, then it was off to Buckeye Lake Music Center in Hebron, Ohio. We did one show there and went to Detroit, to The Palace, in Auburn Hills. This was the first indoor show that I did for the Dead. I saw all of the guys that I had just met the month before and had a great day. The weirdest thing about that day was when I walked out to the front of house in the afternoon, when the arena was pretty quiet, and there was Jay, smoking a huge bong, right in the middle of the arena. I said, "What are you doing, right here, in the middle of the house?" He just laughed and said, "You still don't get it?" I guess at that point it hit me that for the Grateful Dead crew some rules just did not apply. I finally realized that we could pretty much do whatever we wanted to, and there was no one to say a word.

We did two shows at The Palace. On the second show day, we showed up in the afternoon, checked the system, and headed to the bus. As we were sitting on the bus, we noticed that security had shown up with a big nitrous-oxide tank confiscated from one of the fans in the parking lot. They brought it back by the buses and turned it on, to let out the gas. Well, of course, Chuck saw it and grabbed a few balloons that he had on the bus. Chuck and I headed straight over to the tank and filled them up. Chuck then decided that he should turn the tank off, so we could get more in a while. We went back to the bus and started passing around the balloons. We were all just as high as we could be on laughing gas, when we noticed the security guys return and look around to see who had turned the tank off. We were all just laughing away in the bus as they searched for about five minutes and then disappeared. So out we went, filling up the balloons again. This little game of cat and mouse went on all afternoon, until the tank finally dried up.

From Detroit we headed to New Jersey's Giants Stadium. That is a great place to work. The stagehands are great and have been doing shows in there for years. The day went along as well as anyone could expect. When everything was set up, we packed it in for a night of focusing lights. The LD was going to stay till dawn for sure that night. One of my jobs on overnight focus shifts was to make sure that there was always smoke on the stage so that she could see the lights beams to make her looks. Well, as you can imagine, in a stadium the wind is not that predictable. In fact, it changes all the time. The smoke machines that we used for that were

F-150s, and they shoot out a thick smoke that dissipates as it spreads out. I would have to run extension cords all over the stadium to get the smoke to float across the stage. About every half hour, I would have to move the machines to some other place in the stadium. So in between stealing golf carts and doing lines of blow on the bus, you could find me in the stands somewhere moving this machine around. Well, eventually I got tired of having to go through all of the hallways to get up in the stands and back down to the field, so I decided it would be a good idea to just jump over the blue wall that surrounds the field. I saw a guy jump over it once on TV during a football game. So over I went, only to find out that the wall is pretty tall. I just kept falling and falling and wondering what the hell I was going do when I hit. I hit all right, and crumpled into a little ball. Luckily, I didn't break anything, but I sure did feel that for a few days.

After the two shows in Giants Stadium, we headed back home for ten days off. I needed that break. I have no idea how much cocaine, beer, and pot I had consumed over that first run, but when I got home I slept for like two days straight. What a world I had gotten myself into. I had no idea what to expect, but now I had a bigger picture to look at. I really found that I liked this touring business. Finally I had a place that I fit in.

We all collected back together on September 15, 1994, in San Francisco. We played Shoreline again—back to the land where cocaine flows like water down a steam. It seemed like there was a never-ending supply in that venue. With the catacombs that we created out of road cases, it was like our own little cocaine land on stage left. After a night of focusing and piles of our favorite drug, we went back to the hotel for what we called sleep. We had three shows there, and being the home of the Grateful Dead, you could imagine the amount of people all gathered in the backstage courtyard. There is this area backstage at Shoreline where the catering area exists. For normal shows the people leave the area to watch the show, but for the Dead shows that place was its own party within a party. There are televisions that show the stage back there, and in general there was just a mass of people watching and talking during the whole show. If you needed something from catering at that time, you were just out of luck.

An Icon is an automated lighting fixture that is computer driven, and at the time it was Vari-lite and Icon that were the number one choices of lights. As I worked for Light and Sound Design (LSD for short), we owned and maintained the Icon.

One of the days that we were at Shoreline, Phil and I were fixing an Icon. As I explained earlier, we really had no contact with the band, unless it was by accident. Sure enough, that day, as Phil and I were working on the icon, Jerry Garcia came through the upstage left backstage entrance, through the basketball court, and said to us, in that unmistakable voice, "Isn't that one of those lights that move around over our heads?" Tucked into our road case lighting home, no one really had any idea that he was with us. We look at each other a bit surprised, and said yes. Jerry went on to ask how it worked. We asked him if he wanted to see the inside, and he did. We proceeded to take the light completely apart and explain how it works. Jerry seemed very interested throughout the whole process. When it was in pieces and ready to get put back together, he said, "Can I put in back?" We said sure. Well, from step one to step whatever, Jerry Garcia put the whole thing back together. We plugged it in and it started to calibrate up. We got this friendly smile from the man as he picked up his briefcase and walked off. Phil and I just stared at each other and put the light away. Some days on the road just don't seem real, and that was definitely one of them.

We finished the rest of the shows and loaded out until morning. The next part of the tour was way back out to the East Coast, Boston to be exact. The old Boston Garden was the scene for the next week of our lives, and was it ever going to be a few nights to remember.

We loaded the show in as usual, did a show, and stayed all night to focus. Someone got the coke, and we started partying. I know there were a few acid trips in Boston, but to tell the truth, I only really remember four trips on the road, and those came much later. This part of the winter tour was awesome. We had six shows in seven days in Boston. This is also where we began our ritual of searching out Italian restaurants.

There were three of us and sometimes four that started this up. Jay, Phil, Joe, and I began looking for Italian places to eat. In Boston, the place to head to is the North End. Today it is real easy to get to, but then, when the "Big Dig" was taking place, it was a bit of a nightmare. Anyway, we ended up strolling through the narrow, winding streets of the North End, not sure what to expect, except that we were going to get some awesome food for sure. That whole area is Italian. There are so many restaurants in that little part of town, we had no idea which one to choose. After about an hour of walking up and down the streets, looking in windows, we decided that we would try this little place where the road splits and creates a triangle. It was not that crowded, so we asked for a table for three. Of course, we were not dressed up, as no one has any dress-up clothes on the road. They said it would be about twenty minutes. We waited outside and watched several other people show up, without reservations, and get seated right away. I guess with long hair and jeans, we were not welcome.

Just as we are getting pretty mad, this cop comes across the street to the restaurant, which has a line about half a block long, and asks if we are from around here. We tell him no, and that we are having a hard time getting in here to eat. He told us to come with him, and he walked us to the door of another restaurant. He said something to the guy at the door, and they took us straight to a table. We thanked the cop, and he just nodded and said that we didn't want to eat over there anyway.

What a place this turned out to be. The food was probably the best Italian that I ever had. Phil ordered some seafood fiesta thing, which almost filled the whole table. I had some rigatoni, as that has always been my favorite. I don't remember what Jay had. We ordered an antipasto, and soup as well. I'm not sure how we finished all of that food, but we did. The bill was around one hundred dollars. We paid, thanked the cop and walked down the street to the cannoli bakery, had a cannoli and a coffee, and headed back to the hotel.

The weird part of all of this is that each of us, at some point later on different tours, looked for this place to eat there again. It does not seem to exist. When I was on Page and Plant, I took a cab to the North End and asked the cab driver to take me there. He drove right up to the split in the road, and across the street, where we ate, are apartments. I asked him what happened to the restaurant, and he told me it has always been apartments. I had asked Phil and Joe about the place, and they had never found it again either.

The week in Boston went by with the usual partying and goofing off. From Boston we headed to Philly and The Spectrum for three shows. The Grateful dead shows consisted of two sets. They would play for around an hour, leave the stage, then return in about forty-five minutes. During the intermission, we would have to swap out lights that were broken. That meant the whole process of going through channels to get up in the rig. There was not much waiting at this time, though, because everyone knew we had forty-five minutes to get it done. When the call came on the radio, we would have about a five minute-wait for a yes or a no, so we would just put on harnesses and wait for the word.

Well, as my life goes, I was walking behind the stage during the intermission, and a hand popped out and grabbed me. It was Frank and his girlfriend, Amanda, with a huge line of cocaine laid out on a road case. Frank said to dig in and I bent over and snorted as much as I possibly could. Then I leaned over for the other nostril. It was as if an alarm in the world of the gods went off, because as soon as I heaved as much as I could up the second nostril, the radio went off. "Light 535 needs to be swapped." That light was over the stage, and clearance was needed. Frank looked at me and said, "Harness up!" I looked at him. "What? Get Phil, I just put a gram up each nostril." He just shook his head and said, "Harness up!"

Well there I was, shaking like a leaf, with absolutely no control of my limbs, harnessing up to climb a rope ladder twenty-five feet over the stage. The safety equipment would save me if I were to fall, but that was the last thing on my mind. I was worried about doing this at all. The call came through and off I went, sweating bullets as I climbed the rope ladder. It must have taken me three minutes to get up there. I crawled across the truss, holding on as white-knuckled as I had ever been. I got to the light, hooked everything up, and sent the light down to the waiting arms of Frank and Phil (along with about half of the fluid in my body). I got through it, and nothing bad happened, but I promise you I never, ever want to do anything like that again.

There was no time for whining about any of it. I found that no one really cares what you have done to yourself, as long as you can do your job. That was a good lesson to learn, and maybe that is why Frank sent me up. It has come in mighty useful, as time has passed.

We got through the Philly shows and headed to Washington D.C., to the Cap Center, the old home to the Washington Capitals. We loaded that show in, did a show and, as always, stayed all night to focus and program. The next day we showed up in the afternoon, and before long I was handed an eight-ball of coke. I put it away for after the show, but other plans were in order. Before the show ever started, someone whipped out their bag and laid out some lines in our dimmer house of road cases. Once that happens, everyone sooner or later gets into their own stash to spread the wealth. We were all high by the time the show started. I had to sit on stage left by myself during the show to watch the dimmer racks and reset anything if it needed it. Well, the party just kept rolling through the whole show.

When the show was over, I was heading out the doors upstage center, and there were about twenty cops in the hall. Paranoia took over. I was sure they were going to stop me and I was headed straight to jail. With a big bag of blow in my pocket, I headed back to the dimmers and thought through the situation. Needless to say, I was a mess and should not have been trying to think anything through. My thoughts talked me into eating the drugs. I didn't want to waste it, and so in my mouth it went, bag and all. I figured I could swallow it if it got bad. I was soon ready to find out that that was a dumb idea.

I got passed the cops and into the van. By this point, some had come out of the bag, and my whole face was numb. I took out the bag and found that I had a huge mess of melted coke in my possession. I also noticed that the paranoia was getting worse and that I had to get rid of the stuff. I am not exactly sure what I did at that point, but when we got to the hotel Phil stopped me and asked what I was doing that night. No words came out of my mouth except "My room," and off I went. I never got busted, but I sure did get really wasted from all of that coke in my mouth.

The next day Phil asked what had happened, and I told him the story. He sat me down and explained that there was no way any of us on "this" tour was going to get busted by any cops. As paranoid as I was that night, I would have never believed him. But as time passed I began to realize that he spoke the truth. It was an odd tour in that respect, but I guess with the amount of money that was made in those cities, year after year, a few heads were willing to look the other way.

We did the shows in DC, and then came the weird train ride. I say weird only because we had been flying from city to city up till this point. Now all of a sudden we were loading out and the whole crew was headed to the train station to catch a train to Penn Station in NYC. I guess, when I look back, it was pretty smart as far as logistics. We would arrive in the same building that MSG is in and go straight to work. But it sucked for us, the crew. We had to sit up in train seats for the ride, and no one really got any sleep. I think this was the first time that I used coke to get me through the day at work.

We arrived at Penn Station and went straight upstairs to the arena. Everyone was beat and wandering around backstage waiting for the fork-lifts to bring the gear up the five stories so that we could begin to work. As I passed through a hallway with small rooms, there was half of the lighting crew inside doing bumps so that they would wake up. I popped right in and did my share.

The funniest part about doing shows at MSG is that the arena is five floors up from the ground. There is no elevator but instead a ramp that goes around the outside edge of the whole building. I mean it is inside the walls of the building, but it runs all the way around on the outside edges of the interior of the building. I was told that when they had the circus, the elephants would never get in an elevator, so they had to build the ramp. Forklifts collect the gear at ground level and bring the gear up to the arena level. Frank grabbed me right before the forklifts started driving all over the place and dragged me to one of the many columns backstage. Then he ran away, laughing. I was stuck there for about five minutes waiting for a break in the forklift traffic.

Not only is the arena five floors up, it is suspended from the roof. When the crowd stars dancing or jumping, the whole floor goes up and down. It is pretty scary the first time that you feel it because it feels just like an earth-quake. I'm not sure if any patrons ever notice that because they are enjoying the show, but backstage it is very noticeable.

After we loaded in the gear and had everything up, we did a show. The cocaine was flowing before we knew it, and we were all as high as could be before the show was over. When the show ended, we got that dreaded call that we would be staying that night to work on programming. It was weird, because there was really nothing for all ten of us to do all night. We could not do any work in the rig, because it was the union, Local 1, that ran the stage there, and you could not do any of your work without them there to help. Anyway, there we were behind the stage in the hallway inside of our lighting tech area, snorting blow and shooting the breeze. After about two hours of partying and getting completely bored, someone came up with the idea that we should go out to front of house, where they were programming, ask a ton of questions, and just generally get in the way. We agreed that was a good idea; maybe we would get sent home. So off we went to the couch at FOH and plopped right down in the middle of everyone working.

After about twenty minutes of our presence at FOH, Frank looked at us and told us to find somewhere else to hang out. One of us asked, "Like in our hotel?" Frank just gave us a look. We started to ask what he might need us for and why we should stay. It didn't take long before Frank agreed and sent us on our way. He must have seen us talking about one hundred miles an hour and acting all jacked up in front of everyone that had to work.

So Phil and I grabbed the blow that we had bought and decided to head out to the hotel. It was about two in the morning, and we didn't feel like walking down the long ramp, so we just headed out the arena into the lobby. That turned out to be a big mistake. We went through some doors that led to escalators that were turned off. We went down to the next level and found that the doors were locked. So we headed back up the escalator to find those doors were now locked behind us. We found a set of doors that were open and started through the halls again trying to find a way out. Needless to say, we were a mess on blow, arguing and pulling suitcases behind us. A security man showed up. He asked us what we were doing and how we got in there. I'm not exactly sure how we got any real words out of our mouths, but he realized that we were with the tour and took us out to the front of the arena. We got a cab on Broadway and went to the hotel. Phil and I checked in and then proceeded to finish our drugs and talk for several hours. When the blow was all gone, I left his room and headed to mine for my ritual of praying that I would go to sleep sometime before I would have to get up and go back to work.

The next afternoon, I met Phil in the lobby and he looked terrible. We were staying at the Dumont Plaza, which was on Thirty-Fifth and Lexington, just a stroll to MSG. We began walking, and about two blocks into our walk I asked Phil what was wrong. He wouldn't answer at first, but then he let it go. Seems that after I left Phil's room he wanted more blow. He didn't have any, but he knew that Jay had an eight-ball in his workbox at MSG. I guess in Phil's gacked-up mind he thought it would be a good idea to go back to the venue and get the drugs out of Jay's workbox. Phil walked back to MSG, found that same security guy that we had rambled at about two hours before, and talked him into letting him go back to our work area. I am not exactly sure how he was able to function on that level, but apparently he did. He took Jay's blow and went back to his room and did it all. Now he was very upset as to how he would explain what he had done to Jay.

We got to work, and before Jay had gotten to his workbox, Phil pulled him aside and told him what he had done. I guess Jay didn't really want any in the first place, because he told Phil it was cool, just give him some money. Phil was in better spirits for the rest of the day, but he sure did look like a mess. I have no idea how much blow we did together that night, but Phil did a ton more than me. I don't think he ever had time to pray that he would get some sleep. (I did a lot of praying, but I never did get any sleep.)

There were more drugs on our run in MSG, but no more fun stories. On our day off in the middle of the three shows, Phil, Jay, Joe, and I went down to Little Italy and found a great place to eat. I used to keep the business card in my passport, but when I lost my passport years later, that went with it. I can't remember the name of the place, and I'm not sure that it is still there. Little Italy has gotten a lot smaller than it was in 1994, and a ton of those places are gone. The food was amazing, and I ate there on several tours after the Dead.

When we loaded out of MSG, it was the same forklift craziness that was there on the load-in, except down the ramp instead of up. As in all things, going down seems to be much faster than going up. I went down to the trucks to load mine, and at the top of the ramp was Frank, sending me my stuff. We all had lists of what went in each truck and in what order, so anyone could send the gear in order. Although Frank at some point missed a row of boxes, and I had some gear come out of order. I asked the forklift driver to set it down because I could not use it yet, and he yelled at me and said he was going to stay right there until I needed it. Of course, being a little rebel, I found a way to make that the last box to go on the truck. He was right in the way of all of the other forklifts, and they kept driving around him and yelling at him. He would ask me after every box that went in the truck if his was next, and I would just answer no.

As the last pieces went in the truck, I told him that he was up. He dumped the box in the truck, gave me a look that I will never forget, and drove away. As I was getting out of the truck, the Teamster's steward was at the back of the truck. He was a really big guy that towered over me.

The first thing that shot through my head was that I was going to get my ass kicked. Turns out that the guy looked at me and with a chuckle said that was one of the funniest things he had seen in a long time; he couldn't believe that it was a kid that made that guy sit there for the whole truck. I said I was sure that when I got upstairs that the driver would find me and hit me, and the steward told me no one would do anything of the sort and not to worry.

The last bit of fun at MSG happened when we were on the elevator on the way down to street level. Well, I guess actually it was at the airport the next day. The venue was giving away hot dogs that had not been sold, so I took a few for the walk back to the hotel. I was in the crowded elevator, standing next to Amanda, and she had her gig bag with her. The side pocket was open, so I shoved the hot dogs down in there. I guess she never found them that night, but security did at the airport. To this day, I am not sure if she knows it was me that put those in there.

We went home for a break, and the next stop was Denver. We flew on November 28 and loaded in the next day. My flight got in early, as did Phil's, and we went to Hooters to get some wings and some beer. On our way I found a new way of crossing streets. I'm sure that it happens in other places, but Denver is the only place that I know where all of the lights at an intersection turn red, and you can cross diagonally. Maybe not a big deal, but I have always found that really cool, and to this day when I am in Denver I think of Phil and I always cross diagonally.

As I found out, a few beers in Denver, The Mile-High City, is not like a few beers at sea level. We drank about three pitchers of beer and ate a ton of wings. All of a sudden, I was a mess. I was slurring and just about falling out of my chair. Phil just laughed and asked me if I had ever been to Denver. When I said no, he just laughed again and said that we had better get back to the hotel. I was stumbling all the way back, and he just kept laughing and helping me when he could. I crawled into my bed and found that I could not catch my breath and could not sleep. I was used to not being able to sleep because I had cocaine running through my veins, but that was the first time I had not been able to sleep because I drank too much. (In later visits to Denver, I have found that I just don't sleep in the altitude. The beer wasn't actually the culprit that first time.)

The next morning I had the worst hangover I have ever had! I showered and headed down to the lobby, and I just felt horrible. When we got to McNichols Arena, I got out of the van and headed straight to the nearest restroom and heaved. McNichols is an old arena; the ceiling is black and it is very gloomy. The ice floor was down, with homasote over it. Homasote is a fiber wood that used to be laid over the ice in hockey arenas to keep it safe from all of the boxes rolling over it. When it gets old, it gets really dusty; and this stuff was old. There was also a haze of fog that covered the floor from the heat from outdoors and the ice underneath. As my job took place out in the house, I was in the fog and dust all day. All I remember was telling the stagehands what to do and running to the restroom every half hour to puke. From that day forward, I have never drunk any more than one whiskey or three beers in Denver. It is funny to be in Phil's shoes and watch someone who has never been there drink too much. I always try to warn them, but no one believes me...until the next day!

I really wanted to eat buffalo. I had heard that it was very tender, and very good for you. One afternoon, before we went into work, I talked a couple of guys to going to this place called The Rocky Mountain Diner. It is a really neat place on Eighteenth Street. When you walk in, there is a bar that has bar stools that look like saddles, and booths up and down the whole restaurant. We sat down and ordered some artichoke and spinach dip as we looked through the menu. We all passed on the rocky mountain oysters, as I have throughout my life, and went for the entrees. I had the buffalo meatloaf with garlic mashed potatoes. To this day, I still want that dish. It was just to die for. It came out covered in gravy and just fell apart in your mouth. Needles to say, I was sold, and have eaten buffalo every time I get the chance.

From Denver we headed to Oakland. We played the Oakland Coliseum. We stayed in San Francisco and commuted across the Bay Bridge. We did shows on December 8, 9, 11, and 12. On our day off, I hopped on the BART and headed over to Oakland to eat at Zachary's Pizza. There is no trip to Oakland that is complete until you get some pizza at Zachary's. I have had pizza in Chicago, and Zachary's is Chicago-style pizza, and it is unbelievably good. I'm not sure what is in the tomato sauce, but it's the sauce that makes it seem like you are in heaven. After my voyage to eat pizza, I headed back to San Francisco and took a nap.

We all got together and ate at another Italian restaurant, as was the norm for days off now. We found a place up off Kearny Street that had amazing food. I do not remember the name of it, but they served the food "family style," meaning that they served the salad, soup, and appetizers in big portions, and everyone took what they wanted. When the main dishes arrived, we were already full and had to really work to get all of that food down. It was a great meal, and I sure wish I remembered the name of that place. I have been back many times and looked for it, but I have never run across it again.

The shows in Oakland were always crazy. That is really the hometown of the Dead, and it shows. The Deadheads were out in force, and these were the real Deadheads, the ones that started it all! The outfits could have been called costumes as far as I'm concerned. It was a great time for everyone; you just felt the love and peace vibe as if the Dead was just as new and refreshing as it was thirty years ago! Looking back at those shows makes me wonder how we have gotten to the places we are now in this country. It was as if every person in the Coliseum was a friend of everyone else.

We loaded out of the Oakland Coliseum after the show on December 12 and headed to LA. I was living in LA at the time and was pretty stoked to do a show there. We loaded the show into the LA Sports Arena, built our usual room on the side of the stage out of empty boxes, and were hanging out before the show. This was the time that I really found out how much the drugs were of no importance inside the world of the Dead.

As we sat in our little room, someone pulled out a water bong and started to fill it up with pot. I wasn't really thinking about it that much as everyone started to take hits off the pipe and pass it around. I was sitting next to the door of the makeshift room and took my turn as it passed by me. I can't remember who was next, but as I passed the bong to him, I noticed that there was an LA policeman standing right outside the opening to our cave. I think my heart just about stopped as I looked at him. Funny thing was, he just smiled and turned away. At that same point, someone in our group asked him if he wanted some. He just laughed and said "No, I'm working."

Well, of course I just sat there in amazement at that scene. Never in my wildest dreams would I have thought that what I was involved in was as big and powerful as it was. Maybe, thinking back, it was just the time and the place that we were all in. The whole country was good, and the times were all about having a good time. That show traveled around the world and brought the party to everyone. The whole country, it seemed, was a part of that time in a way that I will never see it again. The good times were everywhere, and we were right in the middle of it, everywhere we went.

After the show, we went back to the hotel, The Sunset Marquis. That is still one of my favorite hotels in all of LA. It is nestled just off the Sunset strip on Alta Loma. It is like a little heaven right in the middle of a ton of hell going on just up the hill. We had these awesome rooms with really cool furniture and unbelievably comfortable beds. After we checked in, we all met by the pool to go get something to eat. It was a beautiful LA day, the sun was shining, and it seemed like the whole crew was around the pool. It was one of those moments you will just never forget. I didn't know at the time, but a history of rock legends have spent amazing amounts of time there. I guess that proves the naïve life that I had lived up until this point. Later in life I learned just how famous that place was, but at the time it was my un-famous little home sweet home. If you ever get the chance, just waste the money and stay, you will leave the same way I have every time I have left!

We finished the shows in LA and loaded out. I went from my favorite hotel to my nice little room in the garage. My roommate Cat was still on the road, and, as was the norm, I packed his bong full of weed that I got from the tour, left him a few Dead shirts (he is a HUGE Deadhead), and got a flight to Tampa just in time for Christmas. It was really strange going back there after all of the experiences I had just been through in just over eight months. It seemed as though a whole lifetime had passed since I left. Needless to say, that was just the beginning of my own "Long, Strange Trip."

Christmas was odd. I was pretty strung out, as you could imagine, and was doing my best not to let my mom and family figure that out. I'm not sure if they had any idea how many drugs I was doing at the time, or if they even cared. I think they were just happy to see me come home. I was home for a week or so and was not completely clean. I remember looking up an old Coke dealer that I new and got an eight-ball one of those days that I was home. In fact, I played a round of golf the day I had picked up the drugs and played pretty well.

On Christmas Eve I called up an old friend, Josie, and we went down to Ybor City, to the Castle for a few drinks. She ran into some friends that sold us some ecstasy. We took it and ended up at Track's, which was this gay dance bar. We were dancing when I started to get really out of it. I said something to her, and she said she was feeling really weird as well. We stayed a little while longer, but we were really in a strange place; it was not ecstasy that we were on, that was for sure. We left that bar and sat in her car for a while and just talked. I ran out of smokes, so we drove to the gas station just on the north side of the freeway, between Twenty-First and Twenty-Second Streets. I was at the window when I noticed this guy inside the store and a big guy outside of the store. The guy outside had on a big coat, and I saw what I was sure was a shotgun. I said to the guy at the window that I needed cigarettes, and he threw me a pack.

I must have looked like an alien or something at that point, because I just picked up the pack of smokes, and walked away as if the world was normal. I got in the car, where Josie was waiting, and told her to leave quickly. She did, and asked what was going on. I told I was pretty positive that they were holding the place up, and she said she thought so as well. Somehow she got us back to the Castle parking lot and we both passed out.

We woke up to some guy knocking on the window of the car at around four a.m. He asked us what we were doing and we said we were just talking. He laughed and said that we had been asleep in there for at least two hours and we had better get out of there. We did, and Josie dropped me off at my mom's house. I still was pretty out of it, but got inside and into bed. When I woke up for Christmas, I was a wreck. I felt like I had been poisoned. It must have taken about an hour of dry-heaving in the bathroom before I could face my family. No one ever said anything, we just went on with Christmas as if nothing was wrong.

Well, it was, and that was just the beginning of my life on the road. I had many more things to do to myself on my journey through the world of Rock and Roll. There were going to be many more sick mornings ahead of me. I had just scraped the iceberg. And I was really enjoying the ride.

PAGE AND PLANT

Well I got back to LA after Christmas and settled back into living in my little garage room and partying every night with my roommate. We were drinking cases of beer every night and having a blast. I was still under the impression that I would be going back out on the Dead for the spring tour, so I was just wasting tons of money on blow and beer.

I went on a few excursions out of LA to some of the areas that I wanted to see. I went out to see the huge sequoia trees out east in the Sequoia National Park. I took a picture of myself with the huge General Sherman. I also went to Kings Canyon National Park and went down in a cave there. That started to be a trend for me. When I would start to get really strung out and needed a break, I would pack up my car and head out camping for a few days. This trend would help me get my head back on and slow down the drinking and drugging for a while.

When I got back from one of my camping adventures, I stopped into the shop and spoke with Drake about getting some work. He sat me down and said that I was not going back out on the Dead. I asked why, and he said that they were sending someone else out that had more experience with the electronic lights. He also said that he had something else for me. He said that he needed me to go out as the Icon tech on Page and Plant. I would also teach another tech how to fix the Icons. Additionally, they had a bunch of Kabuki drapes that were going to be around the stage and out in the house. I was to take care of those.

59

I was a little sad to see the Dead come to an end, but to hear that I was going out on the Page and Plant tour was pretty exciting as well. In this business, you find out pretty fast that you can get replaced at any time for any reason. It would not be the last time that I was moving on to something else for a weird reason. I guess you just learn to deal with it.

I guess I was a last-minute add-on as well, because when I got my itinerary my name was not even listed. It was another show that J. L. was the salesman on, so I guess he just found a place for me. He was always really cool about that kind of stuff. Anyway, we flew to Pensacola on February 17 for rehearsals. It didn't take long to find out that this tour was a really big deal. It was the first time that Robert Plant and Jimmy Page had been back together since Led Zeppelin. We started loading in on the eighteenth, and in the midst of that, we went out for dinner with J. L. and a bunch of the crew the first night. Well, when dinner was over and we were walking back to the hotel, we passed a strip bar called Sammy's. A guy on the crew named John slipped off with me to Sammy's.

When we got inside, I started looking for coke right away. I hooked up with this girl and before long she sent another girl over my way. Within the hour, we were on our way to a house to get some coke. We went inside, and there was a huge pile of blow on a coffee table and two eight-balls in bags. There were a few really hot chicks hanging out there as well. We were asked to sit down and have a bit of a party before we took off with our blow. We sat down on the couch and this chick started cutting out lines. We hung out for about an hour snorting lines and hanging with the girls. It was a pretty strange situation, but a lot of fun. After about an hour, I was getting pretty high and asked if I could get a ride back to the hotel. The girl that brought us to the house walked over and said I could stay all night if I wanted to If not, Stephanie would take me back. I opted for the ride, and as we were leaving that girl told Stephanie and I to have a great time.

We got to the hotel, and instead of dropping me off she parked the car in the lot and said, "What room are we going to?" Well, I was pretty taken aback, but way into that! She came up to my room and we partied all night. It was about four in the morning when we finally slowed down the drugs and laid down for a rest. I had to be to work at eight a.m. and knew that was gonna suck. Well, we went at it for a good while, and then I ended up having to go to work in quite the disheveled manner. I left Stephanie there to sleep and wandered over to the venue around seven a.m. My crew chief, Knobby, was there, and took one look at me and said, "You are not supposed to be here till eight." I told him that if I didn't go to work now I would never make it in later. He laughed and let me go about fixing lights on my own.

Around eight thirty a.m. Knobby came by and asked me if I knew where John was. I told him no, and he told me to call him. I did, but he didn't answer his room phone, so I went back to fixing lights. About nine thirty he told me to call John again, so I did, and he answered. I told him he had better get over here to work, and he said he was on his way. Well, that was not the case. He finally showed up at noon. He looked beat, and I imagine he had not been to sleep either. I'm not sure if he had one of those girls with him as well, I never asked. Knobby, on the other hand, was not too happy with John. When John went out to front of house, Knobby just looked at him and said, "Get up in the truss, you have tons of things to fix up there."

John spent the whole day up there sweating, cursing and working. I learned a pretty big lesson about coming to work early, even if you didn't sleep one wink. I was feeling pretty bad around one p.m., and lay down on a box to take a nap. All of the lights were fixed and there really wasn't anything to do. This guy on the crew that I was teaching how to fix lights, Serg, came by and asked me if I was OK. I told him I was fine, I was just coked up with some chick all night and it was catching up with me. He asked me where I got it and if I could get more. I said sure, we could go back that night when we got done.

The rest of the day was pretty mellow for me. Knobby came by a few times while I was just hanging out on the side of the stage. He asked me if I was OK, and I just kept telling him I was fine. Around five p.m. he came by and told me to go back to the hotel and get some sleep. I told him I was fine and could stay, although actually I felt horrible. He insisted that I leave and told me to be back at nine a.m. for work. So I left.

I walked across the street to the hotel and went up to my room. There in my bed was Stephanie. I crawled into bed with her and passed out. I woke up to the phone ringing and a note next to the phone. It was Serg on the phone, and he wanted to go out. The note was from Stephanie; she said she had to work that night but would come by later. It was about nine p.m.

61

and I told Serg I would be ready to go in about an hour. I got up, took a shower, and tried to pull myself together. I couldn't just bail on all my new crew friends, so I got up and got ready to hurt myself again.

Serg and I headed over to Sammy's and ran into the same people I met the night before. We got a table and started to drink. After hanging at the table for about fifteen minutes, the girl from the night before came by and asked if we needed anything. I said "Yes, same as last night." She said it would be a while, but it would be taken care of. About a half hour later, she told us to go outside. Our ride was there. We left and went back to that same house. Well, it was just as it had never changed from the night before, except there were different girls there.

We sat down on the couch again and started getting high. About an hour into the festivities, I started to get pretty paranoid. I'm sure it was the coke, as I had been shoving tons up my nose. I remember at one point someone came in the front door and I was sure there were a ton of guys in uniforms milling outside the house. I hung out for about another half an hour, then said I really had to go. Everyone was having fun hanging out and didn't want to leave to take me back. Anyway, after a good bit of my paranoia kicked in, this girl brought me back to the hotel. I left with another eight-ball and a really big paranoid high. I got back to the room about one a.m. and took a shower, trying to calm down. I did eventually, and around two thirty a.m. I had a knock on the door. It was Stephanie. In she came, and the party began again!

I was pretty surprised that she showed up, but I was pretty happy to see her. We fooled around all night and stayed pretty high. Like the night before, I had to get back to work after no sleep and tons of fun! I left her there to sleep as I wandered back to work around eight a.m.—an hour early again, but I was never gonna sleep anyway. Knobby saw me as I walked in and just shook his head and said there was a pile of lights over there to fix. I went to work.

The day was going really slow, and I was beat. Then around ten a.m. Knobby came over and again asked if I knew where another guy on the crew was. Of course, it was Serg he was looking for. I told him I didn't know where he was. Then came the question: "Did he go out with you?" I didn't want to lie, so I said yes. He just said OK, see if you can find him.

I thought for sure I was going to be in some trouble there. I got on the phone and called the hotel looking for Serg. He didn't answer the phone. I waited about an hour and tried again to no avail. This went on all day, me calling the hotel and Knobby telling me to find him. Around four p.m., Serg walked in the back door and came around the corner where I was working. He looked like a ghost. He was as white as one could be, his eyes as wide as they could get, and he mumbled something about covering for him. I told him that I had been looking for him all day and Knobby was mad. He asked if I would go talk to him, and I told him it would not do any good at this point. About that time, Knobby came around the corner and looked at Serg and just said, "Go to your room, shut off the lights, and go to bed! Come back here at midnight, and you are staying the night shift." Then he walked away.

Serg looked at me and asked if I would stay the night shift for him because he didn't think he would even sleep by midnight. I told him I would, so he went off to find Knobby. Well, about ten minutes later, Serg walked over to me and said he was leaving and that Knobby would not let me cover for him. So I went back to chilling out on the side of the stage.

About twenty minutes later, Knobby came over to me and took me outside. He told me that he didn't know what I was doing to everyone, and it made no sense that I was coming in to work early every day and everyone else was strolling in halfway through the day, but it had to stop. I said, "OK, what do you want me to do?" He told me that I was not allowed to take anyone out with me anymore. If I wanted to sit up and do blow all night and come to work early, that was fine, but no one else was allowed to join me from that point on. I thought that was an acceptable answer, as if I had a choice, and said OK. So I left the gig that evening, crawled back in bed with Stephanie, who was still in my room, and crashed.

She was still there when I woke up and asked what I was up to that night. I told her that I could not go out with anyone anymore. To my surprise, she smiled and said that was cool, she had to run and pick something up and she would be back later. I went back to bed. About three hours later I woke up to a knock on the door, and there she was with a big bag of coke. She said we were gonna hang out the rest of the week alone, no more going out. Well, to this day, I still don't believe that really happened. But it did, and it was a great week. We finished rehearsals and I slept with a beautiful woman the whole week. I could have stayed in that week for the rest of my life and been happy.

Our first show was in Atlanta, on March 1, at the old Omni. I'm glad that I got all that fun in during rehearsals, because my job got horrible really quickly. I took care of six Kabuki drops out in the house and one that wrapped around the whole stage. The one around the stage was fine; my motor points were hung pretty early, so that went up in the air pretty fast. The points for the ones in the house, on the other hand, didn't go so fast. They got hung after everything else—lights, sound, and video. Also, when you get out in the house away from the stage, the steel beams in most buildings become sparse. There are a lot of beams in most buildings above where the stage goes, but the further you get from the stage, there are fewer places to hang things. So my day would finish, if it did at all, right when the crowd was supposed to come in. I spent many days getting yelled at to finish quickly, but by the time I got my motors I could never get all of the work done. There just was never enough time to get it all done.

That went on for the first couple of weeks. We played the Knoxville Bowling Arena, Memphis Pyramid, Miami Arena, Orlando Centroplex, two shows at the New Orleans Lakefront Arena, Austin Erwin Centre, and the Houston Summit before they made the call that we needed to cut all of those Kabukis in the house. I thought my job would go away because of that, but they decided to keep the ones around the stage, and I would help with other things, so I stayed. I sure am glad that was the case, because we were having a blast out there.

The schedule was pretty easy: shows on Mondays and Tuesdays, Wednesdays and Thursdays off, shows on Fridays and Saturdays, and Sunday off. With all of those days off and a crew full of coke fiends, we were in heaven. We were completely out of control with the coke, but somehow kept it together to get the show up and working every day.

After the show at the Summit, we headed to Little Rock for two days off. We stopped at a truck stop early one morning on the way, and Sean and I woke up. Mark was up as well, and Sean and I decided to go inside and get some breakfast for the ride. Mark asked us to get him some French fries. We got off the bus and told the driver that we were heading in to get some food. We walked in the truck stop and headed into the dining area. I asked the hostess where to order food to-go, and she sent us up to the counter. We each ordered breakfast and then some fries for Mark. It was taking a long time for the food, and Sean started to get worried about where the bus was. He asked me to go out and make sure that the bus was still there.

I went outside, and looked at the filling area. The bus was gone. I figured it had pulled over to the parking area, so I went around the building to look. On the other side were a lot of semi trucks, but no bus. I went back inside and told Sean that the bus was gone. The food was still not ready, and Sean got really pissed off at me and told me to go back out there and look again everywhere and make sure. I went back outside and walked the whole parking lot, but no bus! I headed back in, and there was Sean, paying for the food. He saw me shake my head and the look on his face was horrible. I asked the hostess how far away Little Rock was. She said we were about an hour and a half away. As she was explaining this, Sean walked by me, handed me the food, and went straight out the door to have a look for himself.

While he was gone, I set the food on the hostess's counter and told her why we were in town and that I could get her some tickets for the show if she could give us a ride to Little Rock. She explained that she didn't get off work for another two hours, but she would help if she could. I told her that if the bus didn't figure out that we were not on it, I would take her up on that.

Sean came back in screaming at me. He was on a rampage about how that bus driver hated him and left us on purpose. He would not let it go, and I grabbed our food and headed out the door with him following me and screaming. When we got outside, I told him that the hostess would drive us when she got off work, but that was of no concern for Sean, he just kept on yelling. I walked over toward the fence on the edge of the truck stop, near the freeway, took out my breakfast sandwich, and started eating. Sean finally joined me, but he was no fun to talk to. We just sat on the curb and ate, not speaking.

About forty-five minutes later, I saw the bus heading our way from the direction of Little Rock. I told Sean to look, and he just started yelling again, so I left him there and went back into the restaurant. I thanked the hostess and told her that I would still give her tickets for trying to help, but she said that she was not sure if she could go. I got her to give me her phone number (there were no cell phones then, or I would have given her mine) and told her I would call her when we got to the hotel and find out if she needed tickets.

When I got on the bus, Sean was laying into the driver like there was no tomorrow. Mark was trying to explain what had happened, but Sean would not stop. I handed Mark his cold fries, and we both headed to the back lounge. When we sat down back there, Mark told me that he had fallen asleep right after we left the bus to go into the truck stop. He woke up about a half hour later to find the bus was moving but we hadn't given him his fries. He walked up to the front lounge to give us a hard time, and then he realized that we were not there.

He stuck his head into the driver's compartment and, as they were passing an exit on the freeway, asked where we were. The driver said, "Oh shit," as they both read the sign they were passing: Next Exit 30 Miles. Mark said he just laughed and crawled into his bunk, knowing they had to drive thirty miles toward Little Rock before they could even turn around to head back and get us. Mark ate his cold fries with me, and then we both crawled into our bunks for the rest of the ride.

When we got to the hotel, I checked in and called the hostess. She said that she was not going to be able to make it to the show but thanked me for the offer. I gave her the hotel number and told her to call if any of her friends needed tickets, but I never heard from her again. That happened a lot back then on the road. There were so many people that you met and so many people that you spent time with. With no cell phones and no Internet, you lost track of them. They all stay in my memories, some pop up more than others, but they all seem to find a place.

Anyway, we spent two days off in Little Rock and then loaded into the Barton Coliseum. When we arrived at the arena, the truck drivers were all hanging out with this chick in the parking lot. She had black hair and a pretty hot body. A couple guys on the bus started mumbling something about Connie, and that is when it hit me!

"LITTLE ROCK CONNIE"

In the never-dying lyrics of Grand Funk Railroad:

On the road for forty days,
Last night in Little Rock put me in a haze.
Sweet, sweet Connie—doin' her act,
She had the whole show and that's a natural fact.

I got my introduction to Connie later that day after we loaded in, and why not? There is no reason to be a roadie and not be a part of some of the legends! When the production staff showed up, they said that Connie was not allowed to be backstage, and that we were all supposed to keep her out. Well, later that day before the show I saw her in the production office talking away, and no one really seemed to mind.

The show in little rock went on just swell, and off we went for a show in Dallas at the Reunion Arena. From there it was Lexington and the Rupp Arena, then Wednesday to the Cap Center in DC for two shows. Friday the twenty-fourth we headed into Pittsburgh. I had spoken with my grandfather a few days before, and he was going to pick me up at the Park Hyatt after I checked in. I called him when I got there, and he said he would be there in an hour.

When I was young, my mom, sister and I spend at least a week every summer visiting her family. It was always a blast. My grandfather was in the millwrights union for many years and knew a ton of people all over Pittsburgh. I had not seen my grandfather in several years and had no idea how he was doing. I was to find out real soon.

When he pulled up at the hotel, he pretty much drove all of the way over the curb and along the sidewalk. He got out of the car, looking very old. This was such a surprise to me. I had never seen him in such a frail manner. The road is a strange place, and it only gets stranger the longer you stay involved in it. I got in the car, and we drove to his house in Glassport. We spent the day together talking and eating. I saw a bunch of my relatives, and then my uncle drove me back to Pittsburgh. I was glad that he drove me, because I was pretty scared about my grandfather driving back after I had seen the way that he pulled in to pick me up. I have a really hard time saying anything to anyone about their behavior. I guess it is because I know that mine is never that exemplary. I have been accepted by many people anyway. I was however glad that within a few years my mother moved my grandparents into her house in Florida. I'm sure that things would have gone a lot worse if she hadn't.

Anyway, the show in Pittsburgh went well, even though it was in the Civic Arena, with all of that steel hanging from the ceiling, and the bucket trucks were needed to hand-fasten all of the points. From Pittsburgh we headed to Toronto. We had a day off, and Serg and I found a great Indian restaurant for dinner. At some point, at the hotel, someone showed up with a bunch of coke. We did a little that night, but I was way too full to keep that up. I put mine away, which was a rare action for me, and went to bed. We were staying at the Skydome Hotel, which is attached to the baseball stadium, which we were playing the next night. It was really cool staying there; there were windows in the hotel that looked right out over the field.

The next day we loaded in, and that place is huge! The rigging was all pre-rigged, meaning they got the plot ahead of our arrival and hung all of the motors. This was usually the case at that venue, as the roof is so high and the rigging is quite difficult. There were a few points that were not on their marks, and they had to re-rig those points; we were getting pretty far behind schedule. The lighting designer was getting pretty mad and nervous, and a few of the crew were in foul moods, which led to a bunch of arguments. At some point when this was all getting out of hand, I grabbed the LD and took him on the bus. I pulled out the bag of coke that I had put away the night before and we did two big lines each. It was weird, but it worked; we both calmed down and just went into our little "high" and got on with our day. The mood seemed to spread through the crew, and everything started falling into place pretty well then.

From Toronto we headed to Cleveland's Gund Arena for a show the next night. We were supposed to go to Detroit after the show for two days off, but we ended up staying in Cleveland for the next two nights. A couple of the guys in the crew either owned or knew the owners of a bar there and had arranged a party for the band on the twenty-ninth. So after a day off in Cleveland we went to this bar for the party.

It was pretty cool. There was a whole setup down in the basement. We could hang in the bar upstairs on ground level as well as hang in the private bar downstairs. Both Jimmy Page and Robert Plant were there, but they spent the whole night downstairs. At some point I wandered into the restroom downstairs and while I was pissing this guy from the crew asked me if I wanted a bump. I said sure, and after I was done peeing he held out this key with a little tiny bit of white powder on it. I looked at him like he was nuts, as I was used to doing lines the size of my thumb, but it was free, so I snorted it.

Needless to say, not a second after I snorted that bump I grabbed the side of my head and screamed. The pain that shot through the whole side of my head was unbelievable. It seemed as though there was a steady stream of tears pouring out of my right eye at the same time. I looked at him and said, "What was that?" He just giggled and said, "You don't need anymore, that's for sure," and left the bathroom. I sat in there for a minute and started to get this really strange buzz, not a coke high, but a similar speedy high. I pulled myself together and headed back out to join the crowd.

I started to drink more beers, but they didn't seem to have any effect. I just buzzed around the party, with no real ambition to do anything. Before long a few of us got together and decided to go back to the hotel. We thanked everyone and got a cab. I was feeling really strange the whole way back to the hotel and could not tell if anyone else was on what I was on, so I didn't ask or say anything about it. When we got to the hotel room, I just went to my room and sat, not really tired, drunk, or really anything. I decided to take a bath and try to just chill out.

In the tub I could not get comfortable, and all of my skin was pretty itchy. I was scratching and flipping around so much I decided to try and lay down. I got out of the tub, dried off, and lay down on the bed, but it was of no use. I checked my heart, but it didn't seem to be beating really fast or anything. I just kept feeling weirder and weirder.

Before long I decided that the hair on my body was making me itch, so I went into the bathroom and shaved pretty much all of the hair off my body. Problem not solved, though. I remember sitting there in the bathroom scratching all over and wondering how I was going to explain this to the crew the next time we were in one of those team showers after a show.

To make things just a little bit more nerve wracking, we were leaving the next morning for Detroit, and no one would be in bed, as it was a day drive, and I was pretty sure I was going to still be awake.

Morning came around. I threw my stuff that was spread all over the room in my suitcase and headed down to the bus. I sat down in the back lounge, grabbed a beer, and looked out the window. Knobby came in, took one look at me, and asked, "What did you get into?" I replied "A key bump which has kept me up all night." He said, "You, too?"

Seems as though he had a little run-in with the same guy in the bathroom. We sat back there for a while, alone, and talked about the sharp pain shooting through our skulls after we did it and the fact that we were in no way in need of sleep. I felt good, if you can imagine, that I was not the only one on this little trip to the unknown. As we talked, we decided that we were given some crank. It was the only thing that we could think of that would do that. Anyway, we made the ride to Detroit, checked in, and went to our rooms. I remember just sitting in that room for hours; I never left, ate, or slept. We had two shows in Detroit at the Palace, so I didn't check out that next morning. I just got myself and my black eyes out to the bus and loaded in.

About halfway through the day, every day, I would meet Knobby at front of house and he would level the lighting rig. I met him that day, and we both sat on the riser looking like death was right around the corner. He asked if I had eaten; I said no. He then asked if I had slept; I said no. He said he hadn't either. I told him to hold out his hand. We both held out our hands, and they were shaking like leaves. We both just looked at each other and shook our heads. That was some really crazy drug we had gotten into.

We did the show that night, and I went back to the hotel, just so that I could sit in my bed and change channels until we had to check out the next day and head back to the Palace. Not sleeping or eating was not taking much of a toll on me, or at least I thought. I felt really weird but had no desire to eat or sleep. The only real thing that was bothering me was that my hands were really shaking. Knobby was the same way, and I got a little solace in that.

We did the show and loaded out, just to sit on the bus all night staring into space and shaking. That went on all night and into the morning when we got to Philly. We checked in, and I took up my normal sitting in bed, changing channels. And then I woke up to the phone ringing. It was Knobby, saying he just woke up and was so hungry he could eat a cow. It hit me, too, just as he was saying this, and I said I'd meet him in the lobby. I looked at the clock, and it was ten p.m.

We went to the lobby bar and ordered practically the whole menu. The two of us just sat there laughing at each other for about two hours as we ate and drank. When we finally left, I went straight to bed. I got up the next morning, got on the bus, and loaded into the Spectrum. One time on crank should be enough for anyone. I do not recommend even that, actually!

We did two shows at the Spectrum, April 3 and 4. They were uneventful except for the unbelievably stupid load-in and load-out, consisting of the small door, the no man's land, and the fact that there is no place to store anything.. From there we headed to New Jersey and a day off. We played the Meadowlands the next two nights. Every day that we loaded this show in, there were two early calls: one was for rigging, and the next was lighting. I was on the second call, which was an hour after the rigging call. A few lighting guys were in on the early call to run feeder power, set out motors, and run cables to the motors. I had noticed that in the last few venues the stagehands that I would get to help me build the truss and set up the Kabuki system around the stage were keeping a large distance from me. I really didn't think much about it, but today was the day that I would find out what that was all about.

I decided to go in a little earlier that day, because I knew a bunch of the stagehands and wanted to say hello before we started working. As I walked in the big door stage right, I saw a bunch of the hands listening to Knobby, right where I usually collected my stagehands from him every day. I knew a few of the hands that he was talking to, so I kind of just strolled in behind Knobby as he was talking. To my surprise, he was giving them a warning about this guy on the crew that was going to be working with them (ME). I listened as he said, "This guy is gay, and I mean really gay. He will try and rub up against you when you bend over to work, so just keep and eye out. He is a really nice guy, but he has some issues." As he was finishing his little talk about me, one of the hands I knew asked him what my name was, and he said Chris. That stagehand looked Knobby right in the face and said, "You mean the Chris right behind you? Don't worry about a thing, he and I have been gay for years. We all know about Chris and we like him!" Knobby turned about six shades of red. My friends came over and all started hugging me and holding my hand. It was pretty funny. (To set the record straight, none of us are gay, but the whole scene was one of those "to die for" moments.)

From the Meadowlands, we headed to Boston for a day off and two shows at the Garden, April 9 and 10. That was the last year that Boston Garden was used as a venue. It was pretty old, way beyond its years, but it was a great little place and I'm happy to have been able to do so many shows in there. We did the long and tedious load-in and did the show.

During the show, I noticed this amazingly beautiful girl in the crowd. It was as if heaven had opened its gates and let this woman out for the evening. She had long blonde hair, an amazing slim figure, and a smile that just made you melt. She sat in the stands on the stage right side, and as I sat at the dimmers I found myself staring at her most of the night. At the end of the show, I was running around doing my after-show duties, which was basically re-packing the Kabuki system. While I was getting ready to start, I noticed that that beautiful lady was still sitting at the side of the stage in the stands. The lights in the arena were on and a security person was telling her she had to leave. I walked over and said it was OK for her to stay. To my surprise, she wanted to talk to me. We talked for a while, and then I was getting called to work, so I told her I would love to see her in about an hour when I got done and gave her my hotel info. She said she'd meet me at the bar, so I went back to work and later headed back to the hotel, on the bus.

I ran up to my room and hopped in the shower, one of those quick five-minute get-the-scum-off showers, and headed down to the bar. I got a beer and hung out with a few guys on the crew. Well, after about three beers, and an invitation to do some blow, I figured that she was not coming. I left the bar and headed upstairs to a room and did a few lines. I chilled out a bit then and thought I should head back down to the bar just to check. Well, sure enough, as my luck goes, she had stopped by. The guys told me she had a beer and was looking for me. One of the guys said that a sound guy had tried to call my room but got no answer. Of course, I was in another room at the time. I asked where she was, and they said they didn't know. I got another beer and waited, but to no avail, so I headed up to my room for the night.

I got down to the bus the next day and ran into the sound guy that was looking for me the night before. He said that when he could not find me he tried to hook up with her. He took her to his room and took a shower, when he came out she said she wanted to talk to me, not him. She left her number for me and told him to get me to call her that day!

I got to work, got ready for the show, then called the number he had given me. I asked for Claudia, and she said, "Yes, this is she." We talked for a while, and I asked her to come by for the show. She said she didn't want to see it again but would love to talk to me, so I told her I would meet her outside the Garden at nine p.m. after the band went on. When I went outside at nine, there she was, this angel in a long winter jacket with beautiful long blonde hair flowing in the wind. We went to the bus and talked for about an hour. I had to go back to work, so I gave her a key to my room and we could hang out after I got done loading out. She said she would wait, but when she found out I wouldn't be free till two a.m. she changed her mind. She said she would think about it and that I should call her before I left town the next day.

I did the load-out and then got on the bus to go to the hotel. I was thinking there were three scenarios here: I could get back to the room and everything I had with me would be gone; I could get back to the room and there would be no one there and everything as I had left it; or I would get to the room and heaven would have opened its gates again. I was happy with any one of those scenarios, but had my fingers crossed for the last one. When I got to the floor where my room was, I noticed outside my door was the room service tray that I had left on the desk in my room. I opened the door, and the small lamp next to the bed was on, shining just enough light to maneuver through the room. I noticed my suitcase was open and the clothes were all folded up and put away. I looked at the bed, and under the covers was a beautiful angel, dead asleep. I quietly got in the shower and then crawled in bed. Claudia turned over and we kissed, a kiss that would last a lifetime. The memory of that night has a file in my brain forever.

The next morning, I was headed to Florida for a twelve-day break from the tour. We woke up and talked all morning long. I told her that I had to get to Florida for a few days to see my family, but I would get a flight back up later that week to see her. In hindsight, and because I was so new that I didn't know any better, I should have just stayed in Boston. When I got to Florida, I spent two days on the phone trying to get a flight to Boston. Something was going on there because every flight was full. Every person I spoke to from all of the airlines had no answer for me other than there was no way I was getting there this week. I never made it back that week, but I did speak with her a few times after that week, when I was in town. I never saw her again in person, but I will never forget her or the night we spent.

After the break in Tampa, I hopped on a flight to Cincinnati. We started back up again at the Riverfront Coliseum. From there we headed to the Indianapolis Market Square Arena, then on to Chicago. We had a day off, so of course I got some pizza at my favorite pizza place in Chicago, Giordano's. The next day we loaded into the arena and got ready for the show.

About fifteen minutes into the Page and Plant set, everyone and their mother noticed the girl in the front row with huge boobs. Not only were they huge, they were out in the open. We had live video for the show, and the camera guys were all over her. None of the footage ended up on the big screens, but they were getting tons of play in the video room. One of the video guys headed straight down after the show to talk to her, and sure enough, she was back at the hotel later that evening.

We were all partying that night, and when I ran out of coke I got bored hanging out in my room, so I went for a walk. Low and behold, as I was passing through the halls of the hotel, I ran into the video guy and that girl. We talked for a while in the hall, then she asked if I wanted to join them and party a while in his room. I said sure. I sat at the table, the video guy sat across from me, and behind him and off to the side, on the bed, sat the girl. We all did a few lines and took our places back in the same spots. As we were all talking, the girl pulled her skirt up and showed me that she was wearing nothing underneath. We kept talking and she just went to town down there, just out of the view of our host.

As you could imagine, I was getting really hot watching her. Every time he would turn to talk to her, she would casually shift and cover up. She was driving me crazy. Just about the point that I was going to explode, she stared at my crotch and nodded as she mouthed the words "show me some." Well, that turned into quite the episode: me, half naked under the table and trying to keep a straight face as I talked to the video guy, and her, behind him and half naked as well. After about five minutes of that, I finally decided that this was not how I wanted to be caught with him, so I got up and said that I had to be on my way. He shook my hand, and she came over and gave me a hug. As she was hugging me she asked what room I was in, so I told her.

I got back to my room, whiped off my clothes, and jumped in bed, knowing fully well that all I was going to do was stare at the ceiling until the sun came up. About five minutes later, there was a knock at my door, and sure enough, it was the girl. I opened the door, and in she came, taking off clothes and saying how hot it was. Then she threw me in bed and destroyed me. We went at it for about a half hour, and then all of the sudden she jumped up. She said she told the video guy she had to run to her car and get something, so she had better get back to his room. I agreed, we made out for a second, and off she went.

On the bus, in the morning, the video guy was late for the bus call, and then we all saw him coming out the door and kissing her goodbye as he hopped on the bus. I never said a word to anyone about that night until many years later. I still get the giggles every time I think about that one.

After the show that night we headed off to Milwaukee. We had a day off, ate some sausages, and drank beer. There is nothing really great about working in the Bradley Center. It is an older arena, kind of run down, but once we got done working and headed into catering for dinner, the whole world changed. As we got in line to eat, a nicely dressed woman handed us a menu. At first we had no idea what to think, then it hit us as we looked around: they had transformed the old venue into a five-star restaurant. The centerpiece was a mound of ice covered in cold appetizers. There was so much shrimp on one side that you could have hidden under them. There were cheeses, dips, olives—you name it, and it was on that table. They sat us at a table, brought us each a beautiful salad, and then took our orders. I had prime rib, and it was out of this world. In the end we found out that there was a culinary school next door, and they used it as the caterer at a great price. All I can say is, that meal, and every other meal I have had in that building, was amazing.

We did that show and then drove overnight to Minneapolis. We had a show that night at the Target Center. I think that was the first time that I met Mandy and Marsha. They are two stagehands that work for the minneapolis union. What great girls. They are really good at their jobs and are typical Minnesotans in all ways. They have the accent and the hospitality that only comes from up there in the Midwest. Every time I am in town, to this day, I try to reach them.

From Minneapolis we headed off to Kansas City. The riggers on the tour were all from Kansas City, so we were all in for some drinking there. We were out all night; I sure am glad we had the next day off. I spent all of it in bed. We played the Kemper Arena on Friday night, then drove overnight to St. Louis. We played The Kiel Center on Saturday. The Kiel center is a really cool arena, right on the main street in St. Louis. It is down under the ground, and you have to go through all of these strange hallways to get to the arena floor. Once you find your way there, the stagehands are great and the day just cruises by.

From St. Louis we headed to Denver. We had a day off there and played the McNichols arena the next night. From Denver we headed to Salt Lake City for a day off then a show the next day at the Delta Center. The Delta Center is an awesome basketball arena. The ceiling at the time may have been the highest in the country. It was quite an eye opener the first time I walked in. From Salt Lake we drove to Las Vegas for a day off.

It was one of those days off that you never forget. One of the guys on the crew decided to get married that day. This was less of a ceremony and more of a show for the crew and band. We all piled into cabs and headed down to a small chapel where Elvis married couples. The marriage was cool, and I actually spent an evening in an Elvis chapel. We all sat around and joked, but to actually be a part of that is just an experience that is just too cool for school. If I ever get married, I hope the little lady would at least entertain the thought! After the wedding we all headed to the English pub down the street, got hammered, and wandered back to the MGM Grand. The next night we did a show at the MGM. We headed to San Diego overnight for a show the next day at the Sports Arena. After the show at the Sports arena, we headed to LA. Two days off in West Hollywood is just what the doctor ordered.

We all crashed during the first day, then headed out to Barney's Beanery for food. We got pretty drunk and decided to head up to the Rainbow. About halfway up the hill, a couple of the guys decided to leave and go back to the hotel. I traveled along and made it into the Rainbow, but that was about it. I was back in the room about an hour after that.

The next day was pretty relaxed; we went out that night for a few drinks but were in early. We did two shows at the Forum, Tuesday and Wednesday. From LA we headed to Oakland. We had a day off in Oakland on Thursday; we didn't do much, just out to dinner and a few beers. The next day we loaded into the Oakland Arena, right off the freeway next to the baseball stadium. We loaded the show in and got done early. Knobby, Sean, and I decided to take a ride down to Telegraph and check it out. We ended up in some bar and grill. We sat out back, had a few beers, ate some food, then headed back to the arena. It was one of those days where I knew I should not be drinking while I was supposed to be at work, but I was with both bosses, so what could it hurt? We did the show that night and headed to San Jose. We did a show at the Arena and headed six hundred and fifty miles to Portland.

We stayed at the Red Lion in Portland, on a cool road called Thunderbird Way. We goofed off in Portland for two days and did a show at the Coliseum on Tuesday. The Coliseum is the old arena right next to the Rose Garden. It is a really old arena and quite a pain to work in. The Rose Garden was not there then. I have done other shows in the Coliseum, after the Rose

Garden was built, and in the morning when I walk into the old arena and see the Rose Garden next door, I cringe. It would be such an easy day if I were over there!

We arrived in Tacoma on Wednesday morning. We stayed at the Sheraton, on Broadway. We did a show at the Tacoma Dome the next day. The Tacoma Dome is this huge, domed arena. There is a trussing system that comes down from the ceiling and you hang your lighting rig under the one that exists in the room, kind of like in Detroit. But this building is huge! It is a great place to work with tons of room for everything. We did that show, then drove overnight to Vancouver. We played the PNE Building. This was the last show of that leg. We did that show and headed back to our homes.

All in all, that was a great tour; I am friends with many of the guys that I worked with to this day. I got to share some great memories and wonderful experiences. There was talk of doing another leg the next year, but no one knew for sure, so we all said our goodbyes and moved on to the next tour.

THE GRATEFUL DEAD PART 2

June 10, 1995, I got on a plane in LA and headed to Highgate, Vermont. I met up with all of the familiar faces that I just spent the last week with, putting together all of the lighting gear for the tour at the shop in Newbery Park. The next day, we headed to the Franklin County airport, which was shut down for us to do a show there on June 15.

Sunday, June 11, we loaded in at eight a.m. It was one of those long days where we loaded in all day, everyone else left, and the lighting crew stayed all night while the LD, Joe, and Amanda programmed. I came to figure out that when the sun first begins to show up the next day, we would get to leave, no matter what; so in the end we could never be there for a full twenty-four hours. I guess I was always trying to find a good way to look at a horrible day of work.

From June 11 till June 14 our schedule was from dinner until the sun rose. That was never really a bad thing around our crew on the Dead; someone always came up with some type of drug and some outrageous idea of an activity we should all partake in.

The first day of the Dead load-in was always a pain: work all day then program and maintain all night. By the time midnight rolled around everyone was beat. On the eleventh, as always, someone had gotten some coke during the day, and that kept us up the rest of the night. We got a bunch of notes about things that had to be fixed or moved around in the rig and went back to the hotel. A little sleep through the day and back in time for dinner on Monday and another night of programming for them and party-ing for us!

A couple of us had gotten some acid, so when it got to be around ten p.m. or so, we took some and waited for the fun to begin. At some point later that evening, we decided we should go find some golf carts. We grabbed some bolt cutters and headed over to the big shed where all of the carts were parked. Within seconds, we had three carts out and were flying through the grass fields all over the airport. Everyone seemed to join in pretty soon, and the carts were full, all of us hanging on for dear life. With no lights in the fields or on the carts, we were having a blast—until we hit a giant hole and everyone went flying. Luckily no one was really hurt, and those of us that were tripping were laughing so hard we just got right back on the carts and drove them back to their sheds. When we arrived, we saw what a mess we had made of the carts, so we parked them in the back row and left. The rest of the night we just goofed off in the bus, listening to music and tripping. By the time it was time to go back to the hotel, we were all beat, tripping folk as well as straight folk. We had two more days in Highgate, then a show on Thursday the fifteenth. By the time we left there, and pretty much by the time we left any rehearsal space, we were in perfect beat-up form to start a tour.

From Highgate we went to East Rutherford for a well-deserved day off. I slept all day. Around eight p.m. I headed out to dinner. Well, I guess I should say that I went downstairs to the hotel bar for dinner. I had a few beers, ate some food, and saw a bunch of the guys. We all hung out for a while, then I headed in for the night. The next morning we had to load in at eight a.m., and the bus call was at seven thirty. You can see Giants Stadium from the hotel, but for some reason the bus driver headed to the freeway and started driving away from the stadium. I thought Frank was going to rip his head off while he was driving. It took about twenty min-utes to get turned around and back to the stadium. We all went flying off the bus and straight to work. I'm not sure if Frank ever spoke to the driver again. In one of those moods, Frank is not fun in the least.

Working at Giants Stadium is like a dream. The stagehands are great. They just work all day and then ask you what else you need. We got eve-rything set up before the night rolled in, then set up shop on the bus for a night of programming. There was never a problem for the cocaine trade at Giants Stadium, and we all proceeded to snort more than our share. We found golf carts, as usual, and began our races around the underbelly of the stadium. That was great for a few laps, until a door opened up as I was flying through a hallway and I just about took out a stadium worker. I drove the cart back to its parking spot and headed straight back to the bus. If you didn't get caught red handed, you usually got away with the crime. Just to be safe, though, I hid on the bus and got back to snorting lines.

The next day, we showed up around two p.m., started up the lighting system, and went to lunch. When we were at lunch, the FOH crew would run through the system, and about halfway through lunch we would start getting the info as to what lights were not working. After lunch we would go through the whole process of getting access to the stage to fix the broken lights. As much as a pain as it was, we did get to take our time getting ready to climb. After getting everything up and going, we sat back for the show.

We had two nights at Giants stadium, June 18 and June 19. We did the shows and loaded out all night. It was morning before we were done, and leaving the stadium parking lot I saw the biggest mess that I had ever seen. You would think that the loving hippies would be aware of all of the garbage that they left behind, but that was never the case. There was literally garbage covering the whole parking lot, a foot high. To this day, I don't understand that.

That day we drove to Albany, NY. Even though it was a day ride, as you can imagine we drank some beer and slept most of the way. It seemed that when we should have been partying, we were sleeping, and when we were supposed to be working, we were partying. And that was just the way that it would be. The world that I fell into just never seemed to ever mesh with what was going on in the "real world." The real world was slipping away, far away, for me. I was so far away from anything that was remotely real. I was still reading about Native American ways, but even that was being consumed by the outrageous life I was leading. The girls, drugs, and partying were taking away everything I had known as real.

As I look back at all of this, I see that God will allow you to walk down almost any path. He will allow you to look deep into the human cracks that we have made in this world. I have found that some souls need to go deep into what they think they need to find their way back to the Lord. As much as we choose to walk away and explore the unknown, he seems to watch us and wait for the perfect time to pick us back up. Our God is a strange God in so many ways. The love that he shows us really has no boundaries. Somehow he knows exactly what we need to experience, and I was on that path. I am so lucky that he has always been watching and holding me.

We got to the hotel and grabbed some dinner. I must have been beat because when I woke up the next morning I had forgotten to set the alarm. When I got downstairs there was no one around. In those days there was no GPS, so I was on my own to find the arena. I asked for directions and headed out. When I got to the arena, I saw everyone working and thought for sure I would be in a ton of trouble. Just my luck, though, I fell into place and no one seemed to notice at all. I got the trussing and lights up out in the house, as I always did, and we had a great show.

For some reason, I had to store all of my boxes back in a place where, for load-out, I would have to cross the dreaded path of Mr. T. For every show there was a path, marked by tape, from the stage to the backline truck. The rule—fiercely enforced by a guy named Mr. T—was that no one crossed that path until the backline guys were done working and all of their cases were packed away in their truck. That was a dilemma for me, as another rule was that no one could work on stage until the backline guys were packed away, either. That, of course, meant that usually I would get a ton of stagehands to get the lights down from beyond the stage while everyone else waited to work on the gear above and on the stage itself.

So there I was, standing on one side of the path, not able to cross, with twelve stagehands lined up waiting to work. As always, it was taking too long, so I watched Mr. T, and when he turned his back we all pushed cases across the path and to the house. This went on until all of the boxes were past. I know, seems silly, but so many of the rules we lived by on that tour were silly.

We loaded out on June 22, after the second show we headed to RFK, in Washington, D.C. We drove overnight and started load-in at ten a.m. We got everything up and stayed all night to focus lights, as always. I'm not sure what time we left, but when we did we headed to the Watergate Hotel. What a great hotel to stay at. It is just full of history and is beautiful on the inside. My sister came up from Florida to see this show with one of her friends. They stayed with me and were supposed to hang out with our half-sister for the show. Well, that night seems to have been the turning point for that whole tour. Everything started to get a little weirder than the normal weirdness that surrounded the Grateful Dead.

I gave the three of them their tickets and passes, and somehow my half-sister got lost in toon town. My sister came in to the show and told me about that. At some point my half-sister showed up in the production office looking for me, and I got her out to the crowd. My sister lost her again, and we are never really sure where she ended up. My sister ended up riding back to the hotel with me on the bus.

The same day, there was a huge issue in the parking lot. The weather was bad, and lightning was everywhere. There were a few people playing hacky sack, and lightning hit a tree right next to them. Three people were hit, and the news was that at least one had died. But apparently they all survived. One was in a coma for a good while, but she lived.

After that bit of news, we did the two shows in Washington, D.C., and headed to Detroit for two shows at the Palace again. We loaded into the Palace at four a.m. on June 27 for a show that night. Other than the normal drugs and drinking, Detroit was uneventful this time. We did a show on the twenty-eighth, as well, and headed to Pittsburgh's Three Rivers Stadium. We loaded in at ten a.m. on June 29.

I was out on the field, building the "Dead Sheds," which were a bit of a nightmare in the first place. Someone else had done the markings years before, so everyone really had to pay attention to me when we built them or they just didn't go together. When I opened up my box with all of the hardware in it, I found The Blonde Wig. This wig had been floating around for the whole tour, ending up in everyone's boxes. It had turned into a huge joke. We all spent many hours trying to hide it in other people's boxes, and this day was mine.

Well, as we were building the sheds, one of the stagehands kept putting the wrong pieces together and making a mess. After the second time, I told my crew if anyone else did something wrong they would have to wear the wig. Well, within minutes, this same guy bolted a wrong piece together. I grabbed the wig and he just asked, "How long?" I said at least five minutes.

He took it off after five minutes only to screw up again, and I just tossed it back to him. Before long the rest of the crew told him to just wear it until we were done.

About the same time as this happened, Frank called me up to the stage. He asked me why I was making that guy wear the wig. I told him why, and he said that I had to stop because the guy was in charge of the whole local crew. I went back to the local stagehands and told the guy he didn't have to wear the wig, but the rest of the locals disagreed. Therefore, he kept it on, and Frank just kept giving me a hard time on the radio.

That night, we stayed late like we always did to focus, but the upfront steel guys had built a cool bar under the stage this day. I stumbled down there while everyone was working out at FOH. There was an empty seat in between this huge guy named Chuck and this French guy named Stew. They had this gas mask, and they were handing it back and forth. When I sat down, Stew handed it to me and I started huffing away. Nitrous was the fun for the next few hours. They had stolen a tank, and the three of us would finish it. The best part was that I was in the middle of those two, so I got to hit it twice as much. They never even knew, cause none of us was in any shape to think.

My cousin showed up for the show on Friday, June 30. We hung out all show. I remember at one point we were down in the upfront bar and Jerry Garcia walked by in between sets. I thought my cousin was going to fall down. I guess he never realized what I actually did for a living before that moment. He came to many more shows that I worked as they came through Pittsburgh. Then he got married and had a few kids, and the times I saw him dwindled. I'm glad I got to see him as much as I did back then. Maybe I will see him in New Orleans for a Steelers game someday?

We loaded out after the show and traveled to Indianapolis. As I said earlier, this tour started to get really weird, and this next part falls right in line with that statement. This is when the acid trip from the beginning of this book played its role.

After Indy we headed to St. Louis, and there was no question where we were headed for our day off in St. Louis. The same crew headed off to Roxy's around seven p.m. We walked in and grabbed a seat at the stage near the back again. I was hoping that my old friend would be there, but found out soon after arriving that she didn't work there anymore. That place was great anyway. Just the music alone was enough to stay for most of the night.

About thirty minutes into our evening, Jay started to talk with a dancer, Marsha, who had a Grateful Dead dancing bear tattooed on her ankle. We all kind of wandered over there and started talking with her. As it turned out, she had a friend, Amy, that was working that night and who really liked Primus. Jay had told her that I was heading out on that tour after I finished this Dead run. Well, within minutes her friend was out talking with us as well, and told me she really wanted to see Primus when they came through a few months later. I told her that would not be a problem, and she was pretty happy. After we drank a ton of booze at the bar, we left. Marsha had given Jay her number, and Jay said that they were coming to the show the next day.

As was always the case, I was in awe of another dancer. Amy was just beautiful. She was young, with a rocking body and this jet black hair that fell to her waist. I could not wait to chat with her.

They showed up at Riverport before the show. I found a way to hang out with Amy in the back lounge. We talked for about an hour before the show, and then I went to work. When the show was over, they had already left, but Jay told me that they were coming to Chicago and they were supposed to bring him some opium. I was glad that they were coming back, because I never got her number. I could not let that one get past me in Chicago. At least that is what I kept telling myself.

In Chicago, sure enough, before the first show Marsha and Amy showed up. Marsha locked herself in the back lounge and came out with a mound of opium in a plastic wrap. The funny thing was, it was in the shape of her vagina. She had put it up there so security would not catch her. Whatever the reason, it didn't really matter because that opium stayed the same shape until it was all gone. Everyone just kept taking pieces off the mound and leaving the shape intact. I got Amy's phone number and could not wait until I got on Primus so that we could hang out again.

They bailed after the show, on June 8, and we went back to the hotel. On June 9 we showed up around two p.m. We checked everything, as usual, and went to lunch. It was just a normal last day of the tour, for all we knew. We were going to load out and head home. I was going to go do Primus in a few weeks, and then we would all catch up and be back on the Dead in a few months.

That night ended with a recorded rendition of Jimi Hendrix's awesome version of the national anthem and a great fireworks show. I guess that is a pretty good memory of the ending of a crazy tour, and an era that will never again return.

PRIMUS

Primus started out as a great idea, at least I thought. I was going to go out with a few guys from the Dead crew and a guy I met many years ago, Sprout. Sprout and I were stagehands together at the Sun Dome back in Florida. He was in charge of about six spotlights that we had to put up behind the stage. After we got those lights set, we spent the rest of the day working on odd jobs and talking a lot. He is the same age as me, and we ended up getting along really well. When the day ended, he gave me his phone number and told me I was pretty good and that I should move out to LA and work with him. I told him I had to get a few things in order, but by the next time I saw him that I would be ready to head out there. The problem was, before the next time he came through town, my father died. I told Sprout I had to hang out for a while and make sure my mom was OK. He agreed, and I promised him I would go out when I felt she was in good shape. When I finally moved out there, I had lost his number, and I really wanted to get the job on my own, so I never used him to get into LSD.

We ran into each other in the electronics department one day. He said that he had heard I had made it out and that he wanted to work with me on the road sometime. So when I heard that Sprout was the lighting director for Primus and that I would be working with him, I was happy. When I got to the shop to work out what I would be doing, I was told that I would be a lighting tech/carpenter. I was supposed to fly up to San Francisco, meet with the Carpenter and make sure that all of the set pieces would work with our lighting gear.

I flew to San Francisco on July 10 and went directly to Rocket Science, the set company. When I walked in the door I was met with open arms and shown all around the shop. I was going over all of the pieces that would have to fit together with the lighting gear and kept asking where the carpenter was that I was going to be working with. I kept getting answers in the form of introductions. Each new person that I met would show me another part of the set and how it was supposed to work. After about the fifth person, I started to realize that I was the carpenter, and no one else from Rocket Science was going on the tour at all. I started to get pretty pissed off at Sprout and Joe, and within the next hour I called LSD in LA and spoke with Sprout. He told me not to worry and to make sure everything would work and that I knew how to put it all together.

Well, the set consisted of sixteen pieces, three or four travelers, two legs, and an Austrian front curtain. The set pieces were all one-inch-square stock aluminum frames with painted muslin fronts that Velcroed to the frames. The smallest was about 7x7 ft., and the largest was a TV that was about 16x20 ft. The idea with the set pieces was that they were to attach to different carts and roll across the stage. The carts were well designed, and this system seemed to be a great system. The Austrian was a manual rope and pulley system which was all controlled from stage left, and this seemed like it would work well enough. The travelers ran in a trapezoidal shape; they began the show closed, then opened up after a few songs to reveal a beautiful 70 percent drop all the way upstage. It was an airbrushed scene of the ocean and a beach.

After going through all of these details, I was ready to leave. I was still pretty steamed at Sprout, but I was on for the ride. I was supposed to go back the next day to the shop but decided that if they were going to put me in that position I would blow off going to the shop and enjoy a day in San Francisco. I could meet up with the rest of the crew when we loaded into rehearsals at the Warfield on July 12. I called Sprout when I got to the hotel and told him everything looked great, but I was a little concerned about a few things. He said we would sort it all out in rehearsals.

So I blew off going to the shop the next day and spent the whole day walking around the city. I was staying at the Phoenix, which is in the heart of the Tenderloin District. From there I wandered all the way over to the Wharf and around the shore back down Market Street. I spent the whole day just looking at San Francisco life. And a good thing I did, because that relaxing day would be the last one that I would see for a good while.

When I walked into the Warfield, I just about freaked out when I saw how small it was. It is a beautiful old theater in the heart of San Francisco, but it was never made for the show we were about to jam in there. There was no room for all of the band gear, let alone even one of the carts that was supposed to hold the set pieces. I looked at Sprout and said, "Just wait until you see the parts delivered from Rocket Science. They will never fit." It was straight out of *Spinal Tap*. I started to get pretty nervous when the production manager, Dwane, said that everything had to work every day. That meant every set piece, drop, etc.

When the gear arrived from Rocket Science, we all just kind of scratched our heads. We brainstormed like there was no tomorrow. The carts were huge, and as we started to talk about the other venues we were going to play, we knew we had to figure another way to get the props up for each song. The carts would never work anywhere except maybe Universal Amphitheatre in LA. As we started coming up with ideas, Sprout and Joe (a huge mountain climber) decided we should rig some shivs to the upstage truss that held the beach drop, get ropes, and fly them up and down. This ended up being the best solution, but now we would have to store all of the set pieces somewhere on stage so that they would be accessible all show, and maneuverable as well. That turned into quite a task almost every day, as you could imagine. With a bunch of discussions and a whole lot of shopping, we found a way to make it all work. It was not pretty, and some days were really ugly, but we found ways every day—except one—to get it all up for the show.

We got through the rehearsals, packed the trucks, and headed out on the road. None of us slept much during those days; the work was brutal, and we had already started with the coke, so here we go again.

The first show was in Salt Lake City on July 17. We flew in for a completely boring day off on Sunday July 16. If you have never been to Salt Lake City on a Sunday, avoid it for the rest of your life. Nothing is open! Monday, we got on the bus and drove for what seemed like forever way outside of town. Out on the edge of the huge Salt Lake we pulled up to Salt

Air. We walked into this little tiny room through a large garage-type door and just stared at each other. The ceiling was about eighteen feet above the stage, and there was no way we thought we would fit even half the set pieces in that room. As the day progressed, we found a way. We ended up leaving the door open backstage and storing the pieces outside, bringing them in one by one as we needed them. It was almost impossible to explain to the stagehands how to do this job, so Joe and I ended up doing most of the work. This would begin to take a toll on my back as the days progressed. Someone scored a pile of coke, and we sat on the bus as high as we could be watching the go-carts on the track right outside the bus. A couple of the guys on the crew went over to the track and rode, but I just watched.

After the show, we packed up and headed to Denver for a day off. No drinking for me! When we got to the hotel, I was looking through one of the magazines on the desk and came across an advertisement for the Buckhorn Exchange, a restaurant that served buffalo steaks. I had eaten the buffalo meatloaf in the city earlier, and I planned to eat it again, but that steak just look too good to pass up. I hopped in a cab and made my way there. I got a table and ordered a buffalo fillet. After I ordered, I got up and wandered around the place. There was one room that was full of stuffed buffalo heads on all of the walls. In fact, the whole place was filled with stuffed trophies. Running the length of the restaurant was a glass cabinet with birds. There were bobcats, deer, quail, and pretty much every wild animal you could think of in that place. There was one strange stuffed thing up on a huge shelf that I didn't recognize. It was long and cylindrical. When I sat back down to eat the salad that was delivered to my table, I asked about that thing. I was told it was a whale's penis. Whoever I've taken to eat there since then does not believe me when I tell them, but when they ask the staff they always get the same answer.

After the salad, I got my steak and potato. I do not even have words for the meal that I ate that night. All I can say is that if you have the time, find a way to get there! When I was eating, I saw that the light-rail train that ran through downtown had a stop right across the street from front door of the Buckhorn Exchange. I hopped on that train back to the hotel and must have dreamed all night of that meal. I always, always, always eat there if I have a day in Denver!

The next morning we headed out of town and up into the foothills of the Rockies to the famous Red Rocks Amphitheatre. That is one of the most beautiful venues in the world. Being beautiful usually has its setbacks, and Red Rocks is full of them. As the bus pulled up, we hopped off, and the guys that had been there before said, "If you have never been here, you have to walk up the first time." Well, it was my first, and I looked up that crooked road, slanted about seventy degrees, and started. By the time I got to the top I thought I was going to die. There is definitely a first and a last time for that. Since the road is so steep and crooked, the semi trailers can't back up to the stage. In fact, they can't get anywhere near the stage. Everything has to be off loaded to a stake-bed truck and then taken up the side of the mountain to then be unloaded at the stage. Needless to say, it takes a pretty long time for all of that to happen. After getting everything up to the stage, we set it all up and waited for...what? You guessed it. The afternoon storms! The wind kicks up every day at that place. The stage is down a slope between two huge rock formations that act just like a funnel for the wind. With all of the drapes and props, we were in for a crazy night!

The thing about Red Rocks is, the upstage wall is just a bunch of jagged rocks. We flew all of the props in the afternoon so that Sprout could focus the lights on them. They were flying around a bit, but the wind was not that bad. After that was done, we all went down the hill and hung out on the bus for a while.

One of the most intriguing things about Primus is their following. Their fans are very in tune with all of the songs, lyrics, and general feelings of the band. In the song "Hats Off," there is the line "They hosed me down, wrapped me like a bean burrito, then marked the time and date." A fan had chosen to sneak in a few burritos and during that song, he or she chose to heave a few of them at the stage. One hit the red legs (drapes) hanging offstage right. There was a huge bean stripe down the drape from about halfway down to the bottom. After the show Dwane came up to me and said that the band wanted that burrito mark cleaned, and they didn't understand why anyone would try to ruin the set with food. It seemed to me at that point that the fans were even more in tune with the band then the band was with themselves.

Anyway, as the show progressed that evening, the wind picked up. At first it was just a steady, somewhat strong breeze, but within about five minutes the wind turned into a gusty swirl. Joe and I abandoned the props, as they were like sails, and started to watch the ocean backdrop whip around almost into the rocks upstage. Due to the swirling effect of the wind, the drop was also coming way too close to the drummer. We got a call on the headset to go and try and hold the drape down upstage. Joe headed over to stage right, and I headed over to stage left. We both grabbed hold of the drop and held it down as best as we could. Before long, we had both become an extension of the drop itself. We started to fly with the drape, coming very close to the rocks. At that point, the wind was so strong that we had to stay put as best as we could or, for sure, the drummer would be wrapped in the drop. About the same time as this was going on, we noticed that it was really bright upstage; we, ourselves, were really bright. I looked up and noticed that the spotlights were focused right on Joe and I flying in the wind. After the show, Sprout came back laughing and joking about how much fun he had watching us hang from the drop. He said he had to light us; it was the best part of the show. How fortunate for us that our five minutes in the spotlight involved acting like fools in the beautiful, mountainous venue of Red Rocks.

To top all stories off that day, after we loaded out Dwane came on our crew bus and called a meeting. We all gathered in the front lounge and listened to what he said. Apparently, in Salt Air, and in Red Rocks, someone had made their way into the band's dressing room right before the band arrived. There was a huge turd in their toilet, and the water had been turned off so the turd would not flush down the drain. Dwane went off on us, knowing full well that one of us was the culprit. He said when he found out who was doing it they would be going home. Well, we never found out who was dry-docking the band's toilet, but it continued for most of the tour, on random days.

We headed out of Denver on our way to a day off in Kansas City. The best part of playing in Denver is that you usually have a day off on both sides because there is no city close by to play at the next day. So we had a day off in Kansas City at the Drury Inn, and then Friday, July 21, we played the Memorial Hall. At some point during that show, I tweaked my back really bad. Throughout the load-out, the pain ran all over my upper back and straight down both sides of my spine. When we got on the bus to go to St. Paul for a show the next night, I hopped straight in my bunk with a bag of ice, hoping that the pain would leave by that next morning.

When I woke up, the pain was horrible, and I was in a pool of water from the ice I had in my bunk when I crashed. I hobbled into the Roy

Wilkins Auditorium, laid flat on my back, and did my best to direct the load-in from there. Somehow I managed to get my stuff done with the help from everyone else on the crew, but I could barely move. Around five p.m., Dwane got a massage therapist to come in and work on my back. I can't remember her name, but this blonde woman—whom I have seen many times since when I'm in St. Paul—came in and started to work on my back. She said I was a mess and she wasn't sure if she would fix anything, but she would try. She tried, all right, and it hurt the whole time. When she was done, I got up and felt about 70 percent better. I think she is one of the most talented people in her field. I was still sore, but she made it so I could move pretty well for the show and load-out. I got better and better as the night progressed.

From St. Paul, we headed to Milwaukee for a show at the Riverside Theatre the next night. That is one of those old theaters that holds its own in the city. It is beautiful inside but is really hard to work in. The trucks have to back down a narrow alley straight off the main road. There is a small loading dock that attaches straight to the stage. There is almost no room at all, and to make things just a little worse, everything slopes right to the river at the end of the alley. Back then there was just railing at the edge of the river, so you had to make sure that no boxes got away.

We loaded the show in, and ended up, somehow, squeezing everything in. We hung a few of the large prop pieces from the fly rail system, which gave us a little more room to work. By the end of the show, my back was feeling pretty good. As we were loading out on the dock that sloped toward the river, one of the motor boxes we'd stored on the edge of the dock broke free. We chased it, but it was too late. Over the edge, with a huge splash, it went. Most of the motor boxes at LSD have two motors in each, but there are a few with single motors in each. Sprout made sure when we left the shop at the beginning of the tour that all of our motor boxes were the purple, single cases. I am not sure why, but I was glad he had. I'm not sure if anyone ever got in trouble for that, but I do know where that motor is today if anyone is looking for it.

From Milwaukee, we headed to a day off in Chicago. When we pulled up to the Omni Ambassador East and walked into the hotel, Amy was sitting in the lobby waiting. Someone on the crew had called her and told her when we would be there. It was a surprise to me, but as she walked over and gave me a kiss, I could care less about the surprise. Amy had driven in that morning from St. Louis to wait for me. We spent the day walking around Chicago and ended up crashing early. The next morning I left to go to work, and she stayed in bed. She showed up at The Pavilion around four p.m. and we sat outside and talked most of the afternoon until I had to go back to work.

That show was the last one with the Penguin outfits. At the beginning of the tour, when we were in rehearsals in San Francisco, Joe and I got handed the penguin outfits and were told that we needed to wear them while on stage. That seemed like a great idea, until we found that we could not use the carts, and had to fly all of the props. There was no way we could get all of the props around corners and hooked up while we had those bulky outfits on. The solution was that the backline guys would wear them and when they were doing guitar changes, they would waddle out as penguins. That worked out pretty well for a good while. They got really good at it, and it was pretty funny to watch.

But the weird thing going on at shows back then was that the fans started throwing shoes on stage while the bands were playing. It was not just at Primus shows, but shows in general. By the time we had gotten to Chicago, the penguins had to get the shoes off the stage as well as do the guitar changes. The Primus fans had figured out about the penguins, and the word was spreading throughout the fan base. So as the show progressed, the penguins spent almost the whole show waddling around picking up shoes. The fans just kept heaving them out. A few guitar changes were missed, and all of the attention was on the penguins. By the end of the show, Les, the lead singer and bass player, had had enough, and the penguin suits got put away forever.

Amy watched the show, and then, again to my surprise, she came over and said she was leaving. I asked her if she wanted to meet the band, but she just said no, she had to get back and get to work, and she would call me later. I saw her a few more times after that, but before long I stopped hearing from her.

From Chicago, we headed for Detroit. We had a show the next night at The State Theatre. It's another one of the older theaters that are scattered throughout the country. It is right next door to the Fox Theatre. The State has a fly rail system, so we flew a bunch of the props, which always made the

94

day go a lot smoother. That show went off without any hitches. We were getting pretty good at fitting that show into small places by this point.

We headed to Cleveland for a day off after the show. We had a show at the Nautica Stage, which is right on the Cuyahoga River. That river has caught fire something like thirteen times. I know it seems strange, but at one time it was the most polluted river in the United States. The largest of the river fires was in 1952 and caused over one million dollars in damage to boats and a riverfront office building. Anyway, it's a hard place to work, but all day you get to think about that history.

From Cleveland we headed north to Canada, which was always a nightmare with this band. At some point in the history of Primus touring, someone had a water bong on the bus while going into Canada and got caught. I don't think there was any pot in the bust, but from then on there was always a red flag when the band went in and out of Canada. We got stopped at the border, and they went through the whole bus. We were stuck outside in the customs room for about two hours. That sucked, as we had a show that night, July 29, at the Varsity Arena. Two hours of sleep lost just like that! We did that show in Toronto and then overnight to Montreal. When we left Montreal for the border, we knew we would be up again, so we just sat up and drank.

After our two-hour stop at the border, we headed to Boston for a day off. Worcester, to be exact. We stayed at the Clarion Suites, and that was the night we found this Indian restaurant. Sprout was way into Indian food and I kind of liked it, so we all got together and went. The food was awesome. I wish I knew the name of the place; it is just a few blocks from the big arena, but it has been a good while since I have been there. We played the Worcester Auditorium that next night, then headed to New York City for a day off. In New York a few of us got together and went down to Little Italy for dinner. We had a great meal and drank way too much. We all just about passed out on the subway ride back to the Paramount Hotel. The next day we loaded into the Roseland Ballroom.

The current Roseland Ballroom, on West Fifty-Second Street, used to be an ice rink in the '20s, then a roller skating rink in the '50s. It had a tent-like harem décor, and in the '70s it was made into a ballroom dancing hall. In the '80s it was a disco, until a teenager got shot on the dance floor. Now it hosts all types of shows, from parties to rock concerts.

The ceiling was all plaster, and there were only a few places to rig motors for our show. We would never get the show hung with what was there. Before long, the local rigger told us to tell him where we wanted the points, and then he just started smashing holes in the plaster where we needed them. I thought for sure we would be in all kinds of trouble, but no one ever seemed to care. We did two shows there, August 3 and 4. From New York, we headed to the Tower Theatre, in Philadelphia. That was where I finally had issues with the giant prop pieces!

The Tower Theatre was built in the '20s and started out as a vaudeville/movie house. By the '70s it had fallen on hard times and it was bought by Midnight Sun Concerts in '72. This is when they first started doing concerts in it. It is a great house with tons of history. The stage is a bit small, but it has a fly house and we could hang every piece to fly them in and out. The problem with the Tower Theater is that there is no loading door. Everything that you put on the stage has to go through the front door. Everything rolls down the aisle and up a ramp from the floor to the stage. The big TV, even though it was hinged in the middle, would not fit though the door. The stagehands said there was a door in the alley that it might fit in, so we dragged it around, but it still didn't fit. When I told Dwane, he told me to cut it and get it back together again inside. Well that was not going to happen, as that piece was important and after cutting it, it would never be strong again. So I told him no. I guess he found a way to explain why it would not be in the show that night, because I never got in trouble, and I never heard another word about it.

From Philly we headed to Washington, D.C. We played the Bender Arena then had a day off in Atlanta. In Atlanta we played the Fox Theatre. It was intended to be the Yaarab Temple for the Shriners organization. Built in 1929, it fell on hard times when the stock market crashed. It was to be demolished in the '70s, but a few people made a fuss and before long it was named an historical landmark. It was refurbished to its original beauty of Islamic and Egyptian architecture.

From Atlanta, we headed to Fort Mill, SC. We played the Hornets Training Facility, which was this basketball gym with a small stage on one end. The date was August 9, 1995.

We had a guy on the crew, David, who was on his first tour. As it always goes, you get a big head about two or three weeks into your first tour. He was telling everyone, every day, how he did everything out there and we would never be able to do this show without him. That day, it just so happened that he didn't wake up for work. He stayed fast asleep in his bunk, so instead of waking him up we chose to go in and work really fast to get the lighting rig up. We did, and when everything was hung and working, Roy walked out to the side of bus where David was sleeping and hit it really hard several times. It woke him up, and he wandered in rubbing his eyes in a bit of amazement. He was a little scared that we would send him home, but none of us wanted to do his work every day, so we just harassed him all day. He lost his attitude that day and fell right in with us from then on.

That was also the day that Jerry Garcia died. A bunch of us worked on the Dead, including the sound guys. Ultra Sound did Primus as well as the Dead. The sound guys were pretty upset all day, but the lighting guys were happy, as we didn't have to put up with all the rules anymore. As time passed, I missed the Dead more than I thought I would, but that day was a bit of a relief.

That night was one of those nights that you don't forget. Funny things just fell into place one after another.

Almost everyone on the other bus was vegetarian, which made us few guys on our bus vegetarians as well. There really were no vegetarian fast food places then, and for bus food we would always end up with biscuits, gravy, and mashed potatoes from Kentucky Fried Chicken. After about five nights in a row, Roy had had enough. The production assistant delivers the food to us, and as she walked off the bus Roy took one look in the bag and heaved all of the food over her head. A little bit got on her, but most of it went flying across the parking lot. It also just so happened that the promoter, who had just bought all of that food, was walking by and heard Roy scream, "We will not take this anymore!" and slam the door.

The promoter went berserk, as you could imagine, seeing the mess and all of his money basically thrown all over the ground. Dwane had just stepped off his bus at the same time to say goodbye to the promoter, but instead now he had to start explaining our horrid behavior. Within minutes of finishing that conversation he headed straight for our bus. We got yelled at for about ten minutes, and being as mad as he was, Dwane left his production book in the front jump seat of the bus. We pulled out of the venue and headed toward the interstate.

When we were about fifteen minutes into the journey and we had all had a few beers, we got a call on the CB radio from the other bus. Dwane was freaking out trying to find his production book. Of course, we let him worry for a good few minutes. For the record, the production manager's production book is one of the most important documents of the tour. It has all of the info that is needed for every aspect of the production side of the tour—all venue information, all of the contact phone numbers, and all of the advance phone work information is in that book. (And remember, that was in 1995 when the cell phone and computer explosion had not yet taken place, so everything was kept in written form.)

I told Sprout to go get some printer paper out of his backpack. He just smiled as he handed me about fifty blank sheets of paper. I walked over to the hatch that opened up on the roof of the bus, opened it, and told the bus driver to pull ahead of their bus. As we passed by, Sprout held up the production book, opened the binder, and showed Dwane that we had the book. When we got in front of them, Sprout said to Dwane on the CB, "Here you go," and I started heaving paper out the roof of the bus. To this day I don't think anyone knows what Dwane was saying on that radio as papers were flying all over the road in front of him. It took him about ten seconds of screaming until he figured out the papers were blank. He made us pull over and came over to our bus—no words, no eye contact, just stepped on our bus, took his book off the front jump seat, and went back to his bus.

We had a day off in Tampa the next day, and my mom made a huge meal. About seven of us headed there for dinner, and we hung out late eating her amazing chocolate chip cookies until they were all gone! To this day, if anyone is on the tour that I am on and we get near Tampa, they ask if my mom is bringing cookies down to the show.

Tampa still didn't have an arena at that time; in fact, it was quite humorous that we had a hockey team but no real arena in town. Somehow Phil Esposito and his brother Tony found a way to get the NHL to give them a team with no arena, an ice rink that was not regulation, and a facility that only held 11,000 fans. Hats off, boys! The Lightning began their history in the expo hall of the fairgrounds, where our show was that day, August 11.

We did the show in Tampa, and I ran into a bunch of friends that day that were working as stagehands. I was pretty proud that I had made it as far as I had in the business, and all my friends made me feel really good about it as well. My sister and her husband came to the show and met the guys in the band afterwards. They were pretty happy and have told me that many times over the years. After we loaded out, we headed to West Palm Beach for a show the next day.

The West Palm Beach Auditorium is a strange venue. Built in 1965, it has held numerous shows and teams. Today it is owned by the Jehovah's Witnesses, and is referred to by some as the Jehovah Dome. But back then it was a great, strange concert venue. There is a mote around the building with a bridge that the trucks have to cross in order to unload and load them. This puts a damper on getting the truck in for load-out. The fans have use of the sidewalks for a good while after the show as they leave, and they must clear out before you can back trucks in. To tell you the truth, we were not so worried about all of that, because after the show we were headed to New Orleans for two days off. Apparently, in the past the crew and band would head to the Florida Keys to scuba dive, but with the larger crew this year the band didn't want to foot the bill, so they went by themselves and sent us off. We'd meet up again on August 15 for a show at the State Theatre.

We had procured an eight-ball of coke before we left West Palm Beach. We got high until all of the coke was gone, and then drank until we all passed out. We woke up in New Orleans and checked into the Radisson on Canal. I got to my room, and before long Joe called me and wanted to head out and start drinking. We bee-lined it to Bourbon Street and started hitting strip joints. After a few hours of hurricanes and beers, we were a mess. We stumbled back to the Radisson and we both passed out.

The phone rang again a few hours later, just after dark. It was Mary. She said that I needed to get in a cab and meet everyone at the Brazilian themed bar. I told her that I was already a mess and needed to sleep. She said, "Just get up and get here, you will wake up for sure when I gave you what I have." I called Joe, and he was as much of a mess as I was, but we talked each other into getting up and jumped in a cab.

When we reached the bar Mary tossed two capsules in my mouth and told me to swallow. I did and found out that she was given a vile of ecstasy that was meant for the crew in New Orleans while the band went to the Keys. It was some really good stuff from San Francisco, I was told. I had never done ecstasy, so I had no way of knowing just how strange my night would become.

The bar was pretty boring, but everyone kept saying it was early and would get better. I had a few beers but, being as hung over as I was, they didn't go down so well. Joe and I sat there at a table looking pretty bad, until all of a sudden I started to come alive. I started to shake a bit and then I was no longer sick at all. Joe looked about the same a few minutes later, and I said I wanted to get out of there. He was pretty bored there as well, and we told everyone we should leave. They were set on hanging there until the crowd picked up, so we sat for a while longer. After about thirty minutes I couldn't take it anymore, so I just got up and walked out the front door. Joe was right behind me. About four blocks down the road, on my way to Bourbon, I looked back and the rest of the crew was in a straight line, like school kids, following.

We made it to Bourbon Street and ducked into a bar. Dwane bought a round of beers. When he got the bill for all of the nine-dollar beers, he was pissed and said we were all on our own now. We were all hanging out on the corner just outside the bar when I looked down the street and this huge wave of concrete was heading for us. I freaked out and grabbed hold of a pole. Everyone looked at me funny, then all of a sudden we all had a hold on poles. That was when I had the first rush from the ecstasy! I began to realize that we were all in the same plane of weirdness.

The waves just kept coming, one after another with this really cool break in the middle. It was like being high on acid, yet getting a break from the high and being normal for a while in between. I loved this!

After a few waves, someone grabbed one of the girls that was with us and got here to stand on a stool in the middle of the road. Before long, she had her skirt pulled up and people, men and women alike, were slapping her on the butt. That went on for a good while until someone talked her down. At one point I went for a little stroll and made it about two blocks before I hit some kind of imaginary wall and got way freaked out. I hightailed it back to the crew and found that if we all got too far away from each other that would happen. It was really strange. It got to be about one in the morning, and we all headed to the Dungeon.

The Dungeon has many stories to tell. It has a jaded history, as do most places in the old town of New Orleans. What I was told is that it is a vampire bar. At that time, the doors opened at midnight, and the place closed when the sun started to come up. This was around the time when all of the

Anne Rice books were really popular. It says on their Web site that it was a building owned by a Royal Turkish family that was murdered for stealing women and sending them to a dungeon before they were forced into the harems of Istanbul. Whatever the case, the place looks the same now as the night we were there. I'm sure that as times and crowd needs change, the bar will as well. But it is always the vampire bar to me.

When I first walked in, the bartender was pretty gruff and odd. No big deal for us on our drugs, though. We just whipped right passed him and had a look around. I ordered a Guinness and began to drink. After getting my beer, I took a stroll down the bar, and there was Roy. He had not been with us all night and was furious with himself that he hadn't answered the call in his room. There was no more ecstasy left, and he was hammered. Just then this girl, who had been dancing in a cage, walked up to him and said, "I want you to pee on me right here, right now." My jaw about hit the ground! He hesitated for a second, and she just turned around and said, "Too late." He tried to call her back, but she never even looked at him again as she resumed dancing alone in her cage.

I had to pee and was directed to a room that looked like a library. I had to go pretty bad, but the only things in the room were books. I finally started to walk out, and this big guy that worked there showed me the secret book that opened the toilet door. I pissed and went back to meet everyone at the bar. There was a jukebox and someone put on Pearl Jam, something from *Ten*. All of the sudden this girl showed up on the dance floor and started dancing away to the music. We all watched. I ended up next to Joe at the bar. After the song ended, the girl wandered over to the bar by Joe and me, as I ordered another Guinness. She said that was her favorite beer. I bought her one and we talked for a few minutes about Pearl Jam. As the conversation began to slide away, Joe leaned over and asked, "So are you gonna take my friend home?" She said "I sure am," took me by the hand, and dragged me out of the bar, across the bridge, and down some dark alley. We ended up in this upstairs apartment that wrapped around a courtyard in the French Quarter.

I really don't remember much from that point on. I do know that we were listening to Jim Morrison; not sure if it was American Prayer or something else. I also remember having no clothes on in some strange chair. What I remember vividly was when I woke up the next morning.

As I opened my eyes, I knew something was up. The bed that I was in was covered in blood. There was blood on the wall, next to the bed, and I was covered as well. I turned over to see this girl next to me. She had reddish hair and was a little larger than I had remembered. Lots of her skin was all red as well. I got up softly and walked down a hall to find a bathroom. When I found the bathroom, it, too, was covered in blood. As you can imagine, I was pretty freaked out by now. I went back to the bed to make sure the girl was still breathing. She was, so I wandered back to the bathroom. I looked in the mirror and my whole face was red. I washed my face in the sink and then tried to find a way to get out of there. This place wrapped almost all the way around the whole garden in the center of the building. It was door after door of rooms. By the time I found the door to get out, the girl was up and right behind me.

I was a wreck. My head was like mush, and I hurt all over. We started to talk, and she said she had a blast last night. I was in such disarray, I just agreed to everything she was saying. About ten minutes into that conversation, my beeper went off. I called the number; it was a couple of guys on the tour, still awake and wanting to get breakfast at this little French restaurant that they knew of. I told the girl that I had to meet them, and she asked that I call her later that day. I guess I had told her that I was in town for a few days. She gave me her number and I told her I would. I did talk to her on the phone again, but we never saw each other. After breakfast, I headed back to the hotel, showered, and slept until the middle of the next night. I was so beat I thought I might sleep forever.

On Tuesday, August 15, we played the State Palace Theatre on Canal Street. The theater was built in 1926. Hurricane Katrina flooded it in 2005, there were a few shows there in 2007, but then it closed for renovations. Some work was done in 2009, but nothing has been completed as of now.

Everyone had completely destroyed themselves over the last few days, so load-in went quietly and pretty slowly. We did that show and then headed for a show in Houston at the Astro Arena. We then headed to a day off in San Antonio. When we got to the Hyatt Regency, we all headed to our rooms and crashed.

That evening a few of us got together and headed down the Riverwalk. The Riverwalk in San Antonio is really cool. There are sidewalks that run all along the river. There are tons of shops and restaurants. There are also stone bridges that allow you to cross over the river. They are really steep, which allows the little barge-type boats, which are a lot like water taxis, to travel along the river. As we were walking, we passed a place called Dick's Last Resort. We decided to eat dinner there. When we finally got taken to a table, a waiter came by and heaved silverware and a few napkins on our table and never said a word. As we came to find out, the whole theme of this place was to be rude. It was pretty humorous by the end of the meal, because roadies can be quite rude. The insults were flying all over the place by the time our food came. Right after that, the waiter came by and said, "Time out." We kind of looked at him funny and he told us that he had had enough, and we won. I'm not sure how often that happens, but it made us all laugh pretty hard.

In San Antonio we played Sunken Gardens. Sunken Gardens Theatre is an outdoor theater located just south of the Japanese Tea Garden of Texas. It was made into a tea garden by the parks department around 1918. Sunken Gardens is a strange venue, but fine for rock shows. From San Antonio we drove overnight to Dallas. We played the Bandshell on August 19. The Bandshell is a lot like the Hollywood Bowl, without the planets. There are a few of these around the country. From Dallas we went to Albuquerque for a day off, if you can call a 640 mile run a day off. We played the convention center on August 21. From Albuquerque we went overnight to Mesa. We played the Amphitheatre, which is a lot like the Bandshell in Dallas but a bit smaller.

We had gotten the lighting system set up quickly that day, and at some point Roy found a set of golf clubs and balls on the bus. The Mesa Amphitheatre has different ledges of grass in the audience. It is quite a steep hill, so it gives different levels for the audience to stand on. Roy and I started down by the stage and started chipping golf balls up each different level. When we finally reached the second-to-last level, Roy smacked a ball really hard and it headed over the fence. We could not see what was over there, but we sure did hear the glass break. No one was yelling or anything, so instead of hightailing it out of there, we just turned toward the stage.

The roof over the amphitheater is very steep running from the upstage wall toward downstage. Roy looked at me and said he knew he could hit one over the roof with a nine iron. I told him to grab a seven iron just to be safe. Roy just turned from me and whacked a ball with the nine iron. We watched as it soared ever so high toward the stage roof. It really looked as if it would make it, and then all of a sudden it started its downward angle. Roy just missed the front edge and the ball flew straight into the lighting trusses. The backline guys were all on stage working as the loud tingling sound in the trusses began. All of a sudden the stage looked like a herd of large rodents running in all directions. Roy and I did hightail it then, straight to the bus! I really don't remember what was said to us, but we got a reaming from Dwane about twenty minutes after we arrived on the bus. I'm surprised we didn't go home over that one, but then again the way things were rolling on that tour we may have gotten away with anything just short of murder.

After the show in Mesa we went to LA. We had a show that night at the Universal Amphitheatre. I had done several shows there and had gotten to know the local stagehands pretty well. I have always enjoyed working with the head electrician. We loaded in quickly that day; the stagehands are really some of the best in the world. All of our set pieces were hung from stage pipes so there would be no need for us pulling them up with ropes.

The big TV set piece was used in the song "Wynonna has a Big Brown Beaver," and during that song we projected the cartoon-type video from a xenon projector on the TV. While we were bringing in set pieces for Sprout to focus the lights on, I looked up and saw that the piece moving down was going to hit the lens of the projector. Now those lenses cost a fortune, and we didn't have a spare. I ran up the ladder straight across the truss and slapped the piece upstage of the lens in the nick of time. As I caught my breath, I looked down and saw the head electrician standing at the bottom of the ladder.

Well, this was the era when all of the safety regulation started popping up in our industry. In some of the major cities it was mandatory to wear a harness anytime you were above twelve feet. You also needed to hook the harness into a fall arrester when you climbed a rope ladder up to a truss. Los Angeles was one of those major cities. (It has now become mandatory all across the country.)

As I got to the ladder, the electrician held the ladder for me to climb to the floor. When I reached the floor he yelled at me in front of the whole local crew about how I was out of line and that I had just broken every rule in the safety handbook. After about a three-minute dress-down, he asked me to go outside with him. I followed him out to the loading dock, figuring that I was going to be sent to the bus and not allowed back in the building. But to my surprise the first thing out of his mouth was, "Chris, thanks." He said saving the lens was really important. He said he was not going to apologize to me for the yelling inside, because we knew what I had done was wrong and everyone saw me break all of the rules. He did, however, say that he would have done the same thing that I'd done. I'm not sure if that is why we have always been friends or not, but to this day every show that I have worked in that building while he was in charge has been great. I always found time in my day to sit in his office under the stage and talk. That is one of the people I miss in LA. He lives in the South somewhere now, on a huge plot of land. I sure hope he is well.

From LA we headed to San Diego. We played the Open Air Theatre at San Diego State University. That theater is down in a hole. All of the gear had to go down huge steep ramps from a parking lot upstage right. There is an elevator upstage left now, but then it was all pushed by the stagehands. Even with the hard push to the stage, we got the show up quickly.

One of the stagehands was this girl from Canada. She was really cool and got along with all of the guys on our bus. By the time we loaded out, she had found a way to get on the bus for our ride to Berkeley that night.

We all got on the bus that night and had a few beers in the front lounge. I got a little bored and headed to the back lounge. I took a CD out of my CD case and, lo and behold, out dropped a hit of acid that I had gotten on the last Dead run. I stuck it in my mouth, put in a CD, and chilled out in the back lounge. After a couple hours, I was starting to feel pretty good and realized that no one had come back there at all, in all that time. I turned the music off and headed up to the front lounge. When I got up front, I saw that Roy had a huge bag of mushrooms and was holding them to his chest. Everyone looked at me with glazed eyes and asked where I had been. I told them in the back lounge, and asked them why they didn't tell me earlier that they had mushrooms earlier. They said Roy had them hid away and he just brought them out about an hour ago. I told them I had eaten a hit of acid about two hours before, and they all just laughed.

Within the next fifteen minutes we had all figured out that my acid trip was never going to mesh with their mushroom trip. I was just hanging out in the room with them, yet it was as if I didn't exist. This turned into my own little strange trip. I could walk in and around them all and they paid no attention to me whatsoever. I was having a blast. Roy would not let go of the mushrooms, and everyone was trying their hardest to get more from him. This went on for what seemed like forever. I was laughing loudly and making all kinds of ruckus without a single peep from anyone.

We stopped at a truck stop before long, and as soon as the bus came to a stop, all of them flew off the bus and around the store straight to a field in the back. I walked into the store and wandered up and down the aisles looking at everything changing shape. I got to the candy aisle and all of a sudden this thumb lollipop popped right out at me. I picked it up and paid for it. As I was walking back to the bus, the driver yelled at me from the side of the store. He said they were all up in the trees and would not come down. He said we had to leave, but they would not pay any attention to him. I wandered out into the field and yelled at them to get down. All I got was just a bunch of giggles from them. Finally after about the third time, I think Jay said they were staying up there until Dwane came out and got them. I walked over to the other bus and told the guys to wake up Dwane. They argued until I told them why. At that point one of them went back to get Dwane, and the others plastered themselves to the window laughing. Dwane came out dressed nice in his boxers and tank top. He was pissed. He started to yell at me, and I fumbled through enough words for him to figure out I was a mess. Then he just said, "Where?" I pointed to the trees and he headed straight over. He yelled something that I could not understand, then all of the sudden everyone fell out of the trees at once. It was hilarious. They bounced down through branches and hit at different times. They were a mess by the time they got back on the bus. There was blood and tons of moaning. At that point we left.

They were all beat up and hot so they turned the air down really cold. I was freezing, so I got my jacket and my thumb lollipop and sat down to enjoy the show again. As luck would have it, they all got really scared of me and started to call me the devil. So I played with that awhile by putting my hood on and sucking on the lollipop really loudly and making a big fuss about it. That only lasted about two minutes cause they kicked me out and would not let me back in. So headed to the back lounge and chilled out again with my tunes. I stayed back there all night, staring out the window and tripping. No one ever made it back to join me, which was fine with me, actually.

106

We pulled into Berkley and checked into the French Hotel, on Shattuck. Nobody did anything that day until way late. I went with someone to Amoeba Records for a while and grabbed something to eat. I was beat and crashed early that night.

The next day we played the Greek Theatre at Berkley. The Greek Theater is an exact reproduction of the ancient Greek Theatre theater of Epidaurus, built long ago. I studied this theater when I was back in college. I think it is the only one of its kind in the States. It was built in 1903. Being built back then, you can imagine that it is not set up for concerts. They have to bring in a whole staging structure so that you hang the lights. As much as a pain as it is to work there, the BGP guys have such a great attitude that the day goes by pretty easily. It is also pretty cool just to be working in such a cool venue.

From Berkley we headed up to Seattle. The 817 mile ride meant a day off for sure. Most of it would be a submarine ride on the bus, but a well-needed rest after the acid and the Greek Theatre. When we got to Seattle, we pulled into the Camlin Hotel parking lot. It looked like a dump, but as we went to check in, I noticed it was quite elegant. I came to find out that it was built in 1926. It started out as an apartment building, but then was sold to the Vance Lumber Company. Vance added a penthouse to the top, but it didn't work so well and was later converted to "The Cloud Room." The Cloud Room was a restaurant, bar, and a place for live entertainment. Many huge stars of the past played there, including Frank Sinatra, Elvis, and Miles Davis, just to name a few. When we were there, it was a bit run down, but you knew that there was some kind of mystique about the place. In 2003 after a twenty-one-million-dollar renovation, the place is a jewel again.

Joe was living in Seattle at the time, and he took us out to a bunch of the cool "grunge" hangouts. We had a great time that night. Grunge was all the hype at the time, and with Joe living there we got a great tour of Seattle.

The next day we played The Arena. The old arena that we played was in the Seattle Center complex. There are several theaters, a football field, and Key Arena, where the Supersonics played, in that complex. They are is pretty well designed for entertainment. It just so happened that Bumbershoot, a huge Seattle art festival, was beginning soon.

Bumbershoot began in 1971. It was after the World's Fair was held in Seattle, and Boeing was in a depression. Mayor Wes Uhlman, wanting Seattle to be a great American city, needed a solution for the blues that it was suffering. He came up with the idea of a celebration, of sorts, and created a live entertainment/avant-garde festival. Over the years the festival has had its ups and downs, but overall it is still one of the biggest festivals that Seattle has to offer. In 1995, Reel One took over the reigns and opened the festival with a Jimi Hendrix Festival and Tribute Concert. With Jay living there and the tour ending in Vancouver the next night, I decided to stay with Joe for a week and go to the Festival with him and his friends.

We did the show in Seattle and headed overnight to Vancouver for the last show of the tour. We played the PNE Coliseum, which is a small hockey arena on Renfrew Street. The Vancouver Canucks played there from 1970 through 1995. The Vancouver Giants play there now. Everyone was looking forward to the tour being over, and we just pushed straight through the day. After the show, we got back on the bus and headed back across the border through Seattle to a hotel near Sea-Tac. Joe and I had the bus pull off I-5 just near Lake Union, where Joe had an apartment. We hopped off the bus, dragged our bags down Eastlake Avenue to his place, and crashed hard.

When we finally got up, we had some coffee and I met his neighbor, Scott. Scott was this really great guy that was all into smoking pot and enjoying life. Bumbershoot didn't start until Friday, and it was only Wednesday. That didn't matter, though. As I was to find out, Seattle has so many great things to do you don't even need a festival to enjoy it.

As soon as we had our wits about us, Joe decided that we should go kayaking. I had never been, and thought that was a great idea. I asked him where, and he said right across the street; he had two kayaks and Scott had his own. Within minutes we were all crossing Eastlake with kayaks over our heads. I can only imagine how that looked to the people driving by. We dumped the kayaks in the lake just across the street from his apartment in this run-down docking area. From there we headed north up to where all of the houseboats were. We spent hours out there, cruising through all of these neighborhoods of boats. It was amazing to see all of this. I had never in my dreams thought that a place like that could exist.

After the kayaking, we went back to Joe's place and crashed. The thing about touring is, you get tired. At the end of a tour your body is just beat!

The hours and stress add up exponentially. You find yourself sleeping at very odd times for about a week. We woke up later that evening and did a little bit of bar hopping, then crashed again.

The next day we strolled all over Seattle. We were down at the Pike Place Fish Market most of the morning. We strolled through the fish vendors and then through all of the flower vendors and into some craft vendors. We went down some stairs and there was a whole other world underneath. There were restaurants and all kinds of shops down there. I goofed off in a bunch of antique shops looking at all kinds of little trinkets and toys from the past. There are a few great bookstores down there as well. I was pretty hungry and found this place to eat that was a buffet-type place. I had a great bowl of vegetable soup while looking out over the water toward Bainbridge Island. After all of the interesting shopping we did at the fish market, we headed back toward Joe's apartment.

We ended up stopping all over the place on the way back. Before long we had made it up the hill, snaking our way around The Seattle Center, and we were up in Queen Anne. Queen Anne is this great neighborhood up on a huge hill just north of downtown Seattle. There are tons of great shops and restaurants up there, but Joe said I had to have a Dick's burger. We went into Dick's Drive-In and I had a Dick' deluxe, a Dick's special, and a great chocolate milkshake. The burger was nothing amazing, but it was good. Some places like that just have to be frequented. They are town jewels!

After our meal, we headed back down the hill, around Lake Union, and back to Joe's place. Of course we crashed for a long time after that hike. We went out that night and drank, as we always did, and talked all night about Bumbershoot and what bands we wanted to see. That weekend we heard music, music, and more music. It was truly amazing. The list just went on forever. Some of the bands were: Buddy Miles, The Gap Band, Jim Carroll, Los Lobos, Michelle Shocked, MudHoney, No Doubt, Sublime, Vernon Reid, and the Robert Cray Band. It was so cool. I was still way into music, and all of this at once was just a dream. But the two best shows that I can remember were Reverend Horton Heat and The Ramones.

Reverend Horton Heat has always been one of my favorites. I had never seen him live so this was a treat. The venue was strange; it was outside in the park near the big fountain. I think an indoor club is better suited, but it was awesome to just see him finally. On the other hand, The Ramones are always the best show on the planet! I have worked a ton of shows for the Ramones, but this was pretty amazing. They played the big stadium. To tell you the truth, I do not know who else played that particular day. The Ramones stole the show (with a slight edge over the vegetarian burritos that were served by the vendors).

That weekend was one of my favorites of all time. I had been a nobody for years in Tampa, and all of a sudden I was as far away from Tampa as I could get without leaving the US. I was in Seattle in 1995, when grunge was the king of music. I was finally making money doing the one thing that I really enjoyed in life: music. I had worked for two of the biggest bands in history and found a small, fun band like Primus that I fit in with as well.

When all of your dreams start to come true, you tend to forget about your past. The past of church-going was no where near any of my thoughts. I had begun the long hard slide away from God. I was getting ready to find out just how much I could ignore the Lord. Growing up in the church, you never seem to realize that it takes work to be a Christian in this world. It takes time and effort on an individual's part to keep God in the forefront of your thoughts. Praising God seems to drift away as we churn through this society. I was churning away, not only in this society, but also into a world of blatant evil.

I flew back to LA on Monday, September 4, 1995. From that point on, I would be happy. My ball was rolling, and I finally had a career. I took a cab back to Newbury Park, where I was sharing a garage room with a friend, Matthew. I crawled on the couch and passed out.

Matthew was a roadie, too, so we were never really home much at the same time. This time was different, though. He was home, and we had to share. It was not that big of a deal at the time, but looking back, I'm not sure how we didn't kill each other. The room was about twelve by eighteen feet, and all we had in the room was a couch, a small television, and a closet. We were roadies, so we didn't have many clothes and we knew how to live in small quarters, but still it was tight. I think the partying was the only thing that kept it together. I was not scheduled to work again until September 19, in the shop, so we had about three weeks of nothing but drinking and doing coke.

I had a pile of money from the tour and had no problem spending it. The owners of the house liked to drink and party, so we all spent a ton of time doing just that. That first week home, Mathew, the owners, and I must have snorted an ounce of blow. We must have drunk a keg of beer to boot. The best part, so we thought, was that this guy about three doors down was selling us the coke at a great price, and he seemed to have an endless supply. The coke dealer was strange, though, and as the week progressed it got even stranger. He was married and had a few kids. The owners of our place were married as well. At some point toward the end of the week, everything started to get a little uneasy. We were all on edge, and everyone was kind of trying to get away from each other.

That Monday I was crashed on the couch, Matthew was at the shop working, and I heard a knock on our door. I opened the door, and the coke dealer made his way into the room, sat on the couch, and decided to have a talk with me. I was thinking it was no big deal until a gun came out of his pants and he sat it on the little coffee table. He told me that he knew what was going on and if I ever opened my mouth he would deal with me.

Well, I was awake then. He left and I just sat there in a coke hangover trying to figure out what he was talking about. I had some suspicions, but at that point I didn't care what was going on. I'm not sure what he had in mind, and before the day was over I had decided that I was going to move out. Mathew came home from work, and I told him what had happened. I had enough money to leave and told him that I would be gone by the end of the week. He looked confused. We had a few beers that night and crashed early. The next morning before he headed to the shop, he asked me if I minded if he moved with me. I said it was cool and that I would head out to look for a place that day.

I spent the day driving around and writing down numbers of places for rent. I started down in Camarillo and looked all the way to Ventura. It was twenty-six miles north of the shop, but it looked like a cool little town. It is right on the beach. The small downtown is quaint and full of little shops. There were several bars, so I really thought it would be cool to go there. Matthew had a few days off from the shop, and I told him I was going to call a few of the places and go have a look. He said he was in, and we went for a drive the next day. After looking at about three places, we decided on a little townhouse on the corner of Main and Hemlock.

The place was really cool—two bedroom, two bath, and two floors. I was going to pay a little more and take the upstairs. We moved in pretty much right away.

It was awesome. I had this view of the Channel Islands from my bed. As is the case with a roadie's life, we quickly set up shop in no time. By the time I was working in the shop to prep for the next leg of Page and Plant, we had the place just the way we wanted it.

PAGE AND PLANT PART 2

After working in the shop the week of September 18, 1995, I headed out to Las Cruces, New Mexico. We were scheduled for a day of rehearsals and then start this second leg of the tour. The band was down in Mexico finishing up two shows at the Palacio De Los Deportes, then they'd come up to meet us in Las Cruces on the twenty-sixth. We flew into El Paso on the twenty-fifth and met the bus for the ride to Las Cruces. The next day we loaded in and got everything working.

In the midst of working, I was getting really tired of one of the guys on our crew. The whole last leg he had been running his mouth and really getting under my skin. I had realized that it was getting pretty bad, but thought it would pass as all things do on the road. The first show of the tour, at The Pan American Centre, this guy, Flap, just would not stop bothering me. We got through the show and loaded out that night, September 27, 1995.

The load-out at The Pan American Centre is crazy. Everything gets lined up in a big line in the middle of the arena where the center line, in hockey, would be. On each side of the arena there are doors that lead out of the building to where the trucks are parked and ready to load. From the arena floor to the doors is a huge hill. A forklift gets at the back of the line of gear and pushes the whole stack up the hill and outside. You can imagine the mayhem at the top. Boxes have to be wrangled all over the parking lot. As crazy as it was, the load-out didn't take as long as we had expected.

From Las Cruces, we headed to Albuquerque for a day off. Albuquerque is higher in elevation than Denver. I could barely breathe. I don't remember much of that day off at all. The next day we loaded to Tingley Coliseum. Tingley Coliseum reminds me of all of the old arenas in the Southeast. It is one of those arenas that are used mostly for rodeos. It's kind of "earth dirty." The stagehands are really good, so you don't think much about where you are. The only thing bad is that all of the road cases end up covered in the red earth dirt that is in the air.

That night during the load-out, Flap was in rare form. I'm not sure if he was high or what, but he was a hundred miles and hour and running his mouth non-stop. His job was to get the trusses broken apart and sent to the truck. He was in a crazy rush, and no one could slow him down. One of my jobs, during load-out, was to help the dimmer guy, Chuck (the same guy that I had done the Dead with), get the cables off of the trusses and into their road cases. It just so happened that in Flap's rush, he started to throw all of the cables off the truss onto the deck of the stage. Well that was where the problem occurred.

The way that you lay cables on the truss during the load-in is very carefully thought out. Each bundle of cable is laid out in order and placed on the truss or in cable hangers so that they are separate and neat. The neatness is a concern, but the separation is essential for the load-out. Every bundle comes off the truss exactly opposite of the way they went on. This makes for a quick load-out. Well, in Flap's rush he started rolling the cables off the truss and breaking the truss apart. Once he rolled the cables off the truss, all of the cables became tangled and intertwined with each other. Now, to pull the cables meant that every cable would come at you at once. This was not the first time he had done this, but it was going to be the last.

I stomped over to Flap and started laying into him as loudly as I could. Pretty much all work stopped at that point, and everyone was watching. I saw that and turned to walk back to the edge of the stage where I was working with Chuck to pull cables. As I reached the side of the stage, Flap came running toward me and tried to push me off of the stage into the open road cases below. I grabbed him and he immediately ducked down grabbed my shirt. This led to him ripping my shirt down the front. At that point I told him to let go and get back to work. I guess he thought I was going to hit him so he didn't let go. I pushed at him so that we would not be near the edge of the stage anymore and yelled at him to let go again. He didn't, and at that point I grabbed him by his long blonde hair and tried to pull him off me. He kept struggling, and I had finally had enough. I took him by the hair and slammed his face into my knee. He let go and looked up. All I saw was a ton of blood pouring out of his nose. He walked off the stage and straight to the bus, and that was all we saw of Flap for the rest of load-out.

I went back to work, untangling the cables and getting them to Chuck. I then got the trusses broken apart and sent to the truck. When I was finished, I went to Knobby and told him I was sorry about the ruckus, but I had had enough of Flap. He just shrugged and didn't say anything. I figured that I would be going home after that, so I just went to the bus and crashed. I could not imagine that after splitting Flap's nose open I would be allowed to stay out on that tour. I think everyone wanted to hit him at some point, but to take it to physical violence was crossing the line.

From Albuquerque we headed to Denver to play Fiddler's Green. Fiddler's Green was outside of town at that point in history, and it is an outdoor venue. Being September 30, it was quite cold. As we were loading in, we were told that Van Halen had played on the twentieth and it had snowed. Just what we all needed!

Well, none of that was on my mind. I knew that I had to start apologizing to everyone and anyone that I passed. I was sure I would be heading home. I started the day with some of that amazing peppered bacon that catering company used to make. As I sat down to eat breakfast, I apologized to the guys on our crew. They all just kind of blew it off as nothing. After I ate, I started looking for all of the crew chiefs of the other departments. As I was making my way through the apologies, I found that no one really cared. When I finally found the head of the video department, his answer was "Thank god somebody hit him, I think everyone on my whole crew has been holding back."

To my surprise, that was the way everyone felt. There I was, scared that I was getting sent home, and all of a sudden everyone was thanking me, hoping that I had shut him up. I am telling you, this is the weirdest business on the whole planet! As the rest of the tour rolled on, Flap got a little quieter, but there was more violence headed his way. You would think that the fact I wasn't punished for smashing his face would have taught him a lesson.

After the show that night, we stayed in Denver at the Marriott Tech Center. The next day we flew on United flight 1119 to Orange County. We arrived around four p.m. and checked into the Irvine Marriott. There is not a whole lot around that place. We all went to the hotel bar and drank, and then we crashed. The next day we had one of two nights at Irvine Meadows. We loaded in, did the show, and headed back to the Marriott. I wished we were in LA. There is so much to do there and it really sucked just hanging at the hotel. But some days on the road are just that way.

After the two nights at Irvine Meadows, we headed off to Sacramento. Not long after we got on the freeway, all hell broke loose. Everyone was still up and in the front lounge, except for the rigger, Shawny. Someone had just made a fresh pot of coffee. All of a sudden, the brakes engaged—not just a slow braking, but a full-on lock up followed by the bus flying in the air as it hit something with amazing force. You have no idea what it is like being on a bus in the front lounge as this happens. Frightening is not the word. Knobby was standing close to the jump seat and ended up slammed against the front windshield. Chuck was next to the coffee pot and steaming hot fresh coffee covered him. The rest of us were all scattered on seats and the floor. The front passenger tire had exploded on impact, so to tell you the truth I am not sure how the driver kept the bus on the road.

As the bus came to a halt, Flap and I got off and headed back toward the fire that we saw billowing out of an SUV. It was a ways away, and we ran down as fast as we could. When we got to the point where we could make out what was going on, we saw that there were three people in flames inside the vehicle. The worst vision, and I still have it today, is of the person in the back seat clinging to a half-opened window.

As we were trying to help, a policeman grabbed us and asked us what we were doing. We explained we were on the bus that was pulled over up the road, and he told us to go to the bus and he would be up there as soon as he could. In all of this excitement I'm sure we sounded like bumbling fools.

What had happened was, a car had run the SUV into the median, which broke off a piece of concrete that went right into the path of our bus. As the SUV hit the wall, it burst into flames, leaving no chance for anyone inside to survive. Everyone on our bus was OK other than scrapes and bruises and rattled nerves.

Since it was the middle of the night, there was no place for the bus to get a new tire. On top of that, we were right in the "'hood" of LA. As it turned out, a huge tow truck showed up and towed us off the freeway straight down into a pretty scary neighborhood. Before we went to bed, the cops that got us down there to the parking place came on the bus and said we should all stay on the bus. He said there was no reason to be off of the bus in that neighborhood, even in the morning the next day. As I crawled into my bunk, all I could think of was all of the shooting I had heard the last time I was spending the night in Compton. I fell asleep hoping that a stray bullet didn't head into the side of our bus.

The next morning we all woke up and the driver had gotten a bunch of Tamales. They were awesome. We were there till around eleven a.m., waiting for the new tire and everything. We then started on our run up to Sacramento. It would have been nice to have the whole day off instead of riding through the San Joaquin Valley. It is nice, in a way, to see how and where we grow so much food for our country, but it's also as boring as can be. It is a huge valley, crops after crops for hours.

After the long boring ride through the valley, we pulled into the Radisson Hotel on Leisure Lane. Everyone else from the other buses had had a nice rest in a hotel bed, and we had had the scare of a lifetime. I crashed for a few hours and then started to make plans for dinner at the hotel restaurant.

Chuck's wife had driven in to see him, and we were going to go eat together in an hour or two. All was grand until my phone rang; it was his wife. She was really wound up, talking and breathing so hard I could not understand her. Finally I came to realize that there was an issue with Chuck. I heard her say, "Chuck is not breathing, he ate some pills and he is not breathing." I told her I would be right there. Man, what a rush. I got so scared I couldn't even think. I had never dealt with anything that real, and a thousand thoughts were running through my mind. "Oh God, what do I do? How do I explain this? What is the first step? What had he taken? OH GOD!" Things just kept rattling through my brain as I was running through the hotel, trying to find his room. When I found it his wife opened the door a crack and said that he was breathing now.

I just about had a heart attack in the midst of all this, and now he was OK. At that point I wanted to go in and punch him in the face. I didn't, and after she shut the door I walked straight to the bar and started drinking with a bunch of guys on the crew. I'm pretty sure they knew something was up with me, but I never told them what was up. Although time has passed, that was and is one of the scariest moments in my life. Chuck is still good today. I hope he has slowed down a little.

We played Cal Expo the next day, October 6, 1995. During load-in, Flap was up to his antics again, bright and early. The women's bathroom was just upstage center from the stage, and you could see it from on the stage. Flap had decided to make a sign reading "Will's Rest Room." Will was this big strong rigger from Kansas City, and he had had enough of Flap over the tour as well. I think Flap was trying to find some allies at that point, but he was out of luck. Will picked up Flap, in the middle of the stage, in front of our whole crew and also the local crew, and body slammed him. Not only that but he jumped in the air and landed on top of Flap with every ounce of his weight. Flap just lay there for a while, then he rolled over and wandered off the stage. As he was leaving, he grabbed the sign, as Will had instructed, and threw it away. That was pretty much the last we heard of Flap for a good while.

From Sacramento we headed overnight to Shoreline in Mountain View. That is the home of the Dead. I saw all of my friends from the venue and we all talked for a good while over breakfast, in the cool open air of the courtyard. From Shoreline we traveled to Boise and had a day off. The next day we played the BSU Pavilion. It was a brand new venue. We may have been the first act to play there. It has a really low ceiling, and everyone was worried whether we would fit. We did; the lighting rig was a little low, but it all worked out in the end.

The dressing rooms are on the opposite site of the building from the stage. There is a tunnel that runs right under the audience, stage right. Robert and Jimmy had to walk through that tunnel to get to the stage. The noise of the crowd was unreal as the lights went out for the beginning of the show. I was standing near the exit of the tunnel when they emerged, and I wish I'd had a camera because the faces of the two of them, when they heard that noise coming from above, could have spoken a thousand words. There is a video on YouTube somewhere of that show.

From Boise we headed to Salt Lake City. We played the Delta Center. From there we headed east to Chicago. We pulled into the United Center.

This was the replacement for the old, wonderful, Mad House on Madison. It was a huge building in comparison. There were tons of hallways backstage, but the weird part of this is that there is really no level ground back there. All of the hallways are sloped in one way or another. There is no way to leave any boxes on their wheels unless you stick a piece of wood or something under them to stop them from rolling. To this day I really don't understand all of that. You simply have to push all of the boxes from the trucks to the arena floor without stopping, no matter what.

From Chicago we went to Auburn Hills for a day off. We stayed at the Holiday Inn on Opdyke road. We played the Palace again the next day, October 15, 1995. From there we headed to Cleveland and played the Gund arena. The union there is pretty tough. The roadies pretty much are not allowed to touch any of their gear. It makes for a harder day of work for us, but rules are rules, so you get through it. From Cleveland we headed to Montreal. We had a day off in Montreal, which turned into a bit of a nightmare in the end.

Dobbo and I headed out to get something to eat. We ended up on rue S. Catherine. In the '90s that was the entertainment district. Today, there are only a few left, but then pretty much every storefront was a strip joint. We were in and out of all of them. That night of drinking and staring at strippers lasted till the wee hours of the morning. I have no idea what time we got back to the hotel—Manoir le Moyne—but it must have been late. I set my alarm, but I seemed to have set it for thirty minutes before I was supposed to be at the Forum. I woke up in the sunken living room and was completely drunk still. I grabbed everything I had thrown around the room, jammed it in my suitcase, and ran downstairs to check out. Everyone was gone already, and I rushed out the front door and jumped in a cab. I had a few loonies in my pocket and hoped it was enough to get to the forum. Well, I told the French-speaking cab driver that I needed to get to the forum, and he just laughed and said OK. I figured he was just making fun of the American, as was common in Montreal, but in fact he would have laughed at anyone asking for that ride. The Hotel is on De Maisonnveuve, and the Forum is on St. Catherine—one block away. He drove me there and I felt like a complete drunken ass. He didn't even drive around the block. I jumped out, grabbed my suitcase, and handed him all of the coins I had in my pocket. I threw my bag on the bus and ran into the loading dock.

The old Forum has a grand history of twenty-four Stanley Cups, but it also has a history of freezing cold air whipping through the loading dock straight through the building and out the other side. Somehow I just jumped into work as if I was there the whole time, and no one said a word. That day dragged on forever. It was freezing cold all day in there, and I was drunk all day.

From Montreal we headed to Buffalo, back to the old Memorial Auditorium. It was freezing cold, and being right on the river made it ten times worse. The wind was whipping off the river, straight into the catacombs of the winding ramps and up to the arena level. I avoided that all day and just stayed upstairs working. The next day we were at the Sheraton in Hartford for a day off, and then played the Civic Center the next day. That is a strange place. It is attached to a three-level mall. Literally, you walk out the entrance doors to the arena and you are in a mall. It is a straightforward arena, and the day went smooth. From Hartford we headed to Boston, checked into the Guest Quarters on Soldier Field Road, and planned for a good night out.

There was talk of going to the House of Blues to see some band play. They were supposed to be very influential to the music of the time. We were told that we could get in for free if we used our laminates from the tour. It was two guys; one played a sitar and the other played all kinds of weird drums. I have looked it up to find out who they were, but there is no record anywhere that I can find. Anyway, just before it was getting dark, Chuck, a sound guy, and I headed out of the hotel to walk to Harvard Square to try to see the show. As we got to the first corner, Chuck pulled out three hits of acid, and we all contemplated the options. Well, we all know the answer to that one, so off we went on our journey to the stars or wherever we were headed.

It is about a mile walk along the river, and about halfway there, we made a wrong turn. I can't think of any reason that we could have got lost other than the acid. We ended up in some really strange area, quite scary to say the least. As we tripped we just wandered and ended back on track. We got to Harvard Square early and found this Sushi place called Shilla Restaurant. We sat and ordered. The food was amazing. After we were done, Chuck decided to order something called a monkey brain. To this day I think he made it up, and the waitress had no idea what it was either.

Chuck explained that it was a slice of cucumber with a big layer of wasabi on the top. The lady just looked at Chuck with disgust as she brought it over to him. Chuck ate it, all right, and drank about a gallon of water to wash it down. He had tears rolling down his cheeks as we paid the bill and made our way out. I don't know if it was the acid or what, but that was crazy as far as I'm concerned.

We walked across the square and went to the guy at the door of the House of Blues. We told the guy our story, and he must have thought we were out of our minds. He just laughed and said, "No tickets, no entry." By this point we were amazingly tripping. We all just kind of hung outside of the House of Blues and took a break.

Within minutes, or an hour, I'm not really sure (acid has its own ideas about time), a limo pulled up to the front door. Out of the limo stepped Jimmie Page. In fact, long limos kept rolling up and dropping off other rock stars. The last one we saw was Robert Plant. He saw us hanging out by the door and asked us if we were coming in. We told him the guy said we needed tickets; he turned to the guy, said something, and we were allowed in. As we walked by the doorman, he just shook his head.

When we walked in, Chuck and the sound guy took off, and I was standing on the entrance landing looking down at the tables. I saw one seat open and headed there to sit. As I sat and looked around, both Robert and Jimmy surrounded me. That was a sight that I will never forget.

To tell the truth, I didn't last there very long, maybe a half an hour or so. The acid was really kicking in, and there was all this food on the table "melting." I got up from the table and wandered out to the entrance-way, shoved a quarter into a video game, and tried to chill out. At some point I think Robert Plant came by and asked me if I was OK. I said, not now but I will be tomorrow then I hit some kind of wall and just had to leave. I remember walking down along the road next to the river and a limo stopping to ask me if I was OK. I remember saying yes and just stumbling down the road trying to get back to the hotel. Somehow I made it there. When I got out of bed the next morning I remembered this story, and it has stuck with me ever since. I have no idea how much is true or not. I do have a receipt for Shilla Restaurant, so that much did happen for sure. The rest may all just be an acid trip, but I like to believe it was real.

I was a wreck the next day. The Boston Garden had closed that year, and we were in the big, brand new Fleet Center. It was state of the art compared to the Boston Garden, which made the day so much faster. The trucks still had to go up ramps to get in, but you could pull all of the truck into the backstage area now. I searched for the little guy that had blow in the Altoids can, found him, and got a gram. That woke me up enough from my acid hangover to make it through the day.

From Boston we headed to New York City. We had a day off and then a show the next day at MSG. It was the normal forklift fiasco flying up the curved ramp and onto the arena floor. We loaded in, and all went as smooth as it goes at MSG. To this day, all of the horror stories that people tell about working in New York still baffle me. Those Local 1 guys are the best in the country, for real. They always get everything done well and really know everything there is to know about entertainment production. I have learned so much working with them.

The catering room at MSG is up a floor or two from the arena level. You have to cross a hallway where, when the doors are open for the show, the audience has access. After we loaded in, I was working on something at my workbox, and someone came up and started to give me a massage. That was not out of the ordinary, we all worked hard, and everyone needs a little attention now and again. I figured it was my crew chief, and I was almost done soldering whatever I was working on, so I just kept working. After a few minutes, the massage was still going on, and I stopped and turned. To my surprise it was Robert Plant. I asked what he needed and said he could have interrupted me. He replied that he thought I could use a break working so hard, and then he asked me where catering was. I showed him the path and then let him know that he would have to cross through the public on his walk. He then said he would just go back to his dressing room and get something there. That was one of the weirdest experiences I have ever had. To this day I am still surprised that it even happened.

After load-out, the whole lighting crew headed out to a bar down the street from the Barbizon Hotel, where we were staying. We were flying home the next day, and everyone was in quite the spirits for drinking the night away. I was drinking Guinness—I thought, but what I later realized was that the guys were filling my glass half full with port as well.

I was getting really drunk and was trying to find a way to bail and get back to my hotel. At one point I said I was heading to the bathroom, and instead I left the bar. It was raining and I was dashing from door opening to door opening down the streets of New York, when all of a sudden I was tackled by Serg. He and Dobbo grabbed me and dragged me back in the bar. From that point on, they kept pouring shots down my throat and would not let me out of their sight. I have no idea what time we left. In fact, I don't remember much from that point until the middle of the next day.

This part of the story is not my memory, but rather what I was told by Rodney, the backline guy that rescued me. Apparently, I was not down to the lobby the next day to catch the ride to the airport in the town car. Rodney and the moving light programmer, War, were on my flight back to LA. It seems as thought War and I both were not there for our ride. Rodney called our rooms, got no answers, and then got security to go up to each of our rooms. Somehow he talked them into opening up the rooms. He got War up and on his way, and then he went into my room. What he found was a sight for sure. It was about twenty-five degrees in New York that night, and I was found sitting up in my bed, under the covers, with the window wide open. The security guy and Rodney got me up, threw all of my stuff in a bag, and got me dressed and somehow down to the car.

Back then, security at the airport was nothing like it is today. Rodney got us on the flight and into some seats. The planes that were running form New York to LA then were mostly wide bodies with two aisles and seats down the windows as well as seats in the center. The flight was not even close to full, and everyone was spread out all over the plane. Basically everyone had a row to himself, with rows to spare…except for two of us. Somewhere over the beautiful USA, War and I both woke up at the same time to find ourselves leaning head to head. As our eyes met, we jumped away from each other and looked up in the aisle to see the flight attendant asking us if we would like some breakfast. We both mumbled yes and searched for Rodney. Everyone we passed just chuckled. We found him and he recounted the escapade. When I got back to LA I had to catch a puddle-jumper to Oxnard to get back to Ventura. I woke up the next day, in my bed, as sick as a dog. I ended up with pneumonia and was laid up for the next few weeks in bed.

To this day, as I look back at all of the things I put through my body, I am amazed that I still exist. Here is that Grace again. God had found some way to let me survive another round of mayhem. I sat in that bed for a week. I could barely breathe. I did keep feeling a bit better every day, and even though I had a bit of money from finishing that tour, I could not bring myself to go to the doctor. Men are strange that way. We just don't go to the doctor. Someone has to force us. As you can see, I survived and made it on to the next set of adventures.

PRIMUS AND BEYOND

That was the last show that I would do with Page and Plant. I didn't know that at the time, but as I got further into the touring world I found that bands come and go and jobs keep popping up with new bands. I have been very lucky over the years. I have worked with numerous hit bands as well as a ton of older bands. For the first six years or so, I really enjoyed almost everything that I did. What you seem to find is that as time rolls by the whole experience turns into one long day. All of a sudden I look back and sixteen years have passed, and it seems like yesterday that I got in my car and drove to LA. You always hear how bands can't believe that they have been playing together for thirty year; well, those thirty years just feel like one really long day. There is something new just around the corner, and the time between is just your nights. Time to rest and get rejuvenated for your next run.

Touring for rock bands is a strange way of life, to say the least. Some of my fellow crew members are brothers for life. I'm not sure if they feel that way, and I know it is not like that in the present, but the guys I worked with back then will always have a place in my life. I would meet a few more on the journey, but for some reason the first two years on the road are as clear as glass in my mind. No matter what happens in life or where any of those guys end up, they know they can call me and I will find a way to help as best as I can.

After those first two years, the days started melting together and the highlights began to be the only things I remember. I thought about ending this book when the day-to-day memories stopped, but I found I had more of this story to tell.

So here we go on the next jaunt of my journey. It starts in my place in Ventura. I got a phone call from the production manager from Primus. He started to tell me how the crew was going to change. Joe was going to be the LD and run the lighting console, which meant I was going to be in charge of the whole set, with a new guy under me. Joe and I had come up with all of the ways to get those set pieces to work for the show, and I knew I had a little leverage to get some more money. As I said back before the last run, I was kind of bamboozled into this carpenter job in the first place. I remember there were a few phone calls after I started with him about wanting more money, but in the end we worked it out and we both seemed to be happy.

The rest of the crew would change as well. Sprout was leaving to do something else, Tack was coming out to be the dimmer guy, and Cheeto was to be the crew chief.

Well, the new guy working under me, Fred, was a certified rigger who has gone on to make a great career at Kish Rigging. When I look back, I was a complete jackass toward him most of the time. He knew so much more than me, and I should have listened to him more often. Anyway, we did find a way to work together and had a great run. After a few years on the road, every single person seems to go through a period where they think that they are great, that no one can challenge them, and that they are irreplaceable. I was there!

We started the tour in Davenport, Iowa, at the Parker Arena, November 10, 1995. From there we went to Indianapolis and the Pepsi Center. The next stop was the beautiful Fox Theatre in Detroit. What a gem of all gems. That theater is one of the most amazing places in the world. The lobby is unbelievable. Huge columns made of marble and beautiful staircases that should be in a museum. It is like walking into a new universe. The stage itself is small, but the grandeur that the audience walks into and then sits in is to die for. The history alone is worth a study. The artists that have graced the stage are innumerable. (Which led me to wonder what in the world Primus, with its enthusiastic audience, was doing playing there. Not that I minded; I got to spend a day there that I will cherish for a lifetime.)

From Detroit we headed to Kalamazoo for a day off. The next day we played Wings Stadium, then we went to Dayton Ohio to the Hara Arena. On November 16, the band taped the Conan O'Brien show, and the rest of the crew had a day off in Beaver Falls, PA. As you can see, the days are really melting together. Mixed with shows and days off, we went to Albany, Buffalo, Hamburg, Danbury, Bethlehem, Uniondale, Baltimore, Hampton, Athens, Winston Salem, Orlando, Pensacola, Nashville, Louisville, Springfield, Madison, and finally Denver, on December 10 at the Coliseum.

There were some great stories, but they didn't seem to come as frequently as they had as in the past. You just fall into that traveling or working groove and days just keep passing by. One of the best stories took place all tour long. Tack and Cheeto take the lead role in this one.

Tack was an amazing technician. He could fix anything. He had worked in the electronic department at LSD since he was in high school, and he had a huge head to go with it. Plus he was anal about everything. Just before the tour, he had a new workbox made, and on tour he would set it up by the dimmers, stage left, every day. The top of the workbox flipped up and would actually face the crowd. With all of his ranting and raving about knowing everything, we all started to pick on him. This is typical on the road; you get bored so you find ways to entertain yourselves. Tack became the target, and he would get pretty mad. He was quite the homophobe, and I found a great way to wind him up weekly. When he would flip his box up, I would write in white gaff tape I AM GAY on the lid. This would face the crowd all night, and by the time he closed it up at the end of load-out, he would see it and go through the ceiling. I got away with it more times than not, and I'm not sure if he ever figured out who was doing it. That is the thing about touring, if you are a jerk all of the time, the way Tack was, you have way too many people wanting to take the piss out of you to figure out who did what.

One day I needed a wrench to fix something, and I asked Cheeto to hand me his wrench. He was on the floor by the dimmers and grabbed one out of Tack's workbox. I fixed the problem and threw the wrench in my pocket. By the time I had finished load-in, I had forgotten that I had Tack's wrench. I was on the bus and getting ready to take a nap when I noticed that I still had it in my pocket. I walked out to the front lounge, where Cheeto was, threw him the wrench, and asked him to put it back when he went back in the building. He told me to put it back myself and dropped it on the table. Well, Tack, being as anal as he was, had cutouts for every tool in every drawer of his workbox. By the end of the day he knew his wrench was missing, and he made a huge fuss during the whole load-out. I knew the wrench was still sitting on the table in the front lounge of the bus, and I just watched as he spun himself all evening. When we got to the bus, I handed him his wrench and he yelled that I would have to put it back where it came from. I told him Cheeto had handed it to me, so if he wanted it back in its little home, Cheeto would have to put it back. Days went by with the wrench floating around the bus. Finally at one point, I put it in the bunk that Tack and I shared as a junk bunk (a bunk that no one sleeps in, where you put bags and things that you need on a daily basis). It stayed there the rest of the tour, but Tack was unaware and kept yelling at me every day. It got to the point where he told me I would have to buy him a new one.

On the last day of the tour, after the load-out in Denver, we were cleaning out the bus at the hotel, and Tack pulled out his wrench from his side of the junk bunk. I started to laugh, which sent him over the edge. He jumped at me and pushed me straight back to the back lounge of the bus. To stop him I put him in a headlock and sat on the seat. He would not let go of me, and Cheeto came in yelling at me to let him go. When we finally parted from the skirmish, neither one of us spoke to each other.

Tack had this huge backpack that he had all of his stuff in. He was not that big, and I never knew how he could carry such a big bag, but he did. We were all on the same floor of the hotel, and as it turned out Tack and I ended up in the elevator together, alone. We didn't say a word, and when the door opened he took off quickly in front of me. I saw him open his door, a good thirty feet in front of me, and then something happened. I don't know how, but somehow he lost his balance and ended up falling backwards into the hallway. He was on his back like a turtle trying to get back to his feet. I passed by him and didn't even laugh as I said, "Serves you right." From that day on he was Turtle Boy to me.

There is another story from that Primus tour, this one from Pensacola, FL. We played the Civic Center, which was where I did rehearsals for Page and Plant a few years before. Sammy's, the strip joint is right down the road from the arena. Everyone had been to Sammy's, and we decided to load in really quickly that day so we could head over to Sammy's for the afternoon. We accomplished that, and while at Sammy's we found some girls who had the evening off and wanted to see the show. So we left them tickets and passes at will call when we got to the arena.

The Meat Puppets were the opening act on that tour. Before they took the stage, Joe called me on the radio from front of house and told me he saw security keeping the girls from going to the arena floor, even though they had passes. He asked if I would go get them and bring them to front of house.

That is where the problems started. I guess the security guy didn't want us to have the local girls with us. When I got to him, he said he didn't care what passes they had. The girls were not getting by. I called Dwane on the radio, and he said that they could get through. That was no answer for the security guy, and as I went to hand him the radio to talk to Dwane, he was "struck" with my radio antenna. That was it! He called someone on his radio, and I could hear that the cops were coming. I called Dwane and said he had better come out to the arena because I was being escorted backstage and they said I was going to jail. Dwane showed up just as we had gotten across the arena floor and they started to push me pretty hard through the doors. He asked them to stop and talk, but they were on a mission. He got in front of one of the cops, and they told him it was none of his business and he should leave. Well, I had a huge set change to do and he knew it, so he told them I was not going anywhere without him. They said, "Fine," in a very nasty tone.

The next thing I knew we were in some room with a huge table and this big cop sitting there. They pushed me into a chair and everyone sat. There was this little meeting between that big cop and all the other cops, and they talked real quietly. Dwane and I could not hear a word they were saying. When that ended, I was told that I was being arrested for assault with a radio antenna. I was sitting there thinking about how anyone could get hurt from a hand-held Motorola radio, when Dwane said that that was ridiculous. They told him to shut up; he had no room to talk, since he had tried to steal a cop's gun. Well, that was when I figured we were in trouble. This whole story was made up. No one was there to straighten any of it out. Dwane called the promoter and told him where we were, and that's when both of our radios were taken away.

We could hear the Meat Puppets finishing up their last few songs, and I knew I was going to be late for set change if I didn't get out of this mess. The promoter showed up, but things took a while before everyone calmed down enough to sort through it all. With a bunch of talking on all sides, they decided to let me go, but I had to give up my radio for the rest of the show. Dwane made a fuss and told them he would not let the show happen if they didn't do something to the security guy as well. The cops told Dwane that there would be a show with or without him. What they didn't know was that Dwane mixed the PA and there really would not be a show if he didn't get out of there. The security guy ended up outside the arena watching the trucks. I got let out and went to the stage. I have no idea what happened after I left that room, but Dwane was in there for a while.

When I got to the stage, the set change was half done. Cheeto was screaming at me for being late and that because I was late we would hold everything up. I tried to tell him what happened, but he thought I was making it up. I also told him that Dwane was with the cops now and we could not start without him. Dwane got out of there and to front of house about ten minutes late. Cheeto didn't believe anything I said until after the show on the bus.

What we came to find out was that the cops didn't want the kids from the stands to jump the wall and get down to the floor. They were very worried that this would start a full-on riot with way to many people on the arena floor. The audience that Primus has is known for its rowdy behavior. They throw shoes, jump walls, mosh, and basically let loose. I can understand the police wanting to keep control, but when the lights go out, the kids do what they want. The kids jumped the walls and the cops tried to stop them for a few minutes and then just gave up. It was a nightly occurrence. What the police didn't seem to understand is that the kids take care of each other pretty well. They don't tend to hurt each other; they just seem to act the part. The show went great and no one was hurt.

Years later, I was in a House of Blues with another show. I was standing outside the elevator doors when they opened and Les Claypool and Dwane exited. They had come to see the show I was on and say hello to some of the crew. Dwane said hello, and we spoke for a while. He asked Les if he remembered me from the earlier tour and he said, "How could I forget?

You almost took my production manager to jail." I guess being remembered for something is better than not being remembered at all.

That ended a whole chapter in my touring life. I caught the tail end of everyday pirate life. I'm glad I got to LA when I did, because all of that crazy day-to-day silliness was about to come to a halt. I'm not saying that the pirate way of life ended, it just started to change.

Much later on, I became good friends with a guy, James, that ran the electronics department for LSD. He had toured years before, mostly with Blue Oyster Cult. He was from Pennsylvania. He had a background in theater, and ended up in Rock and Roll. He toured for See Factor, which is still around today. No one will forget the first time they see those bright orange boxes. James taught me a lot as the years passed. One of the conversations we had, in a bar of all places, was about how touring has changed over the years.

James and I spent more than our fair share of time drinking in bars. The conversation about touring was one of those lessons you keep under your skin forever. He started by explaining that there were three generations of roadies at that time. I had always thought that there were two, but as he explained there really were three. The first generation was the guys that he learned from; they were mostly guys from the Vietnam War, and carnies that found a way to fit in doing road work. His generation was next, and the stories he has are legendary. Then there was my generation. My generation had the crazy stories, but we would have never had the time for all of our goofing off if it was not for the second generation setting it all up for us.

James went on to school me in the facts from when he was out on the road. He was the head electrician and had many more responsibilities than the guys have now. Back then, the tour hired the lighting and sound company, but the companies had to get paid by the local promoter directly. James would have to work all day setting up and tearing down, then go into the show settlement and get paid for the lighting system. For weeks, he would sleep on thousands of dollars under his mattress on the bus until he could find a bank to deposit the money into See Factor's account. The only saving grace was that the technology was nowhere near what it is now. I'm not saying that he didn't spend his share of days buried in a dimmer rack trying to get it working for the show, but at least he didn't have fifty moving lights on top of that.

There was also the fact that an itinerary didn't exist back then. James told me that they knew what city they were heading to next, but a lot of times they had no idea where they were playing. Talk about Pirate Life! He told me of how they would pull into a city in the morning and start asking where the band they were working for was playing that day. If that didn't work, they would buy a newspaper and start searching from that. Then they would have to figure out where that venue was. Today you pretty much know where you are playing without an itinerary. There are only a few venues in each town. But back then, who knew what warehouse you may have been going to? A lot has changed since then, and we all have those guys to thank.

As I said, things started to change. I was put on R. Kelly as a moving light tech. LSD had the gel scroller and moving light account, but RA Roth, out of Atlanta, had the account for everything else. Two of us from LSD, Tony and I, headed out to that tour and joined the RA Roth crew. First of all, LSD was the best and biggest lighting company in the world at that time. Going from an LSD crew to the RA Roth crew was a major change. I don't think Tony and I would start working until three or four hours into load-in any day on that tour. Those guys were really slow, but then again, as I look back, that is were where they were at the time. Everyone wanted to work for LSD, and those that didn't work there had to work somewhere.

The tour started on April 4, 1996, in Rochester. Rehearsals started a week before that. Tony and I had known each other from the shop, but we never worked together on the road before. As was always the case back then, we decided to go out for some beer one night during rehearsals. Rehearsals were horrible; we were working non-stop and we needed a break. One night we met in the lobby and headed out. We walked down the street and were trying to decide which bar, of the few that were open, we should go in. Finally, after passing up a few, we wandered into this bar. We ordered a drink, which we really needed, and then had a look around. No chicks! We looked at each other and started to put it together: yep, gay bar. Oh well, neither one of us cared, so we finished our beers and left. We then went into the next bar: gay as well. We had a beer there and made our way to the next. Well, we must have been in "that" area of town, because, as you guessed, we were three for three. At this point we could care less and just sat at the bar and drank. The bartender was great and we ended up spending about two hours in there laughing. There were guys dressed up like women, then they broke out into Broadway numbers. They were not even working. They were just hanging in the bar with us. Well, that was a night to remember. We ended up hammered, and as we were leaving, everyone in the bar started throwing condoms at us and yelling, "It's not just us that need to be careful!" Needless to say, it would be a long time before we were to have any more fun like that night out there. We basically stayed drunk for the next ten weeks.

That tour sucked! Almost everything about that tour sucked. There was a whole entourage that followed R. Kelly around, and that was a disaster. I think they may have had two buses or more full of people that had no jobs out there. Every day was a nightmare. The mornings would be normal, but around lunch, when all of those people started to wake up and filter in, it just got horrible. They would head into catering and eat all of the food. It turned worse at dinner. Tony and I just started eating a huge breakfast and skipping lunch. But there was no way to make it through the night without dinner, so we would find a way to get in right when they first started serving, hoping we'd miss that crowd.

I think it was Memphis where the shit actually hit the fan. I got into catering that day, and there was a choice of steak or fish. Usually it was chicken or fish, but that day it was steak. I grabbed a huge steak and went to the side of the room to eat. About halfway through my meal, the entourage made its way in and started to raise all kinds of hell as to where the chicken was. The catering staff said they didn't have any; it was steak or fish today. Well, with all of the screaming and yelling, someone had to scream out that the crew must have eaten all of the chicken and that we had no right to do that. A table with a bunch of food went over at one point, and I was pretty happy I had gotten there early. I found all of this quite amusing, but the production manager didn't. What happened at our next stop, Chicago, on April 23, was great.

We had a day off, and then when we loaded into the UIC Pavilion, the whole entourage was sitting in the stands watching us work. No one on our crew had any idea what was going on. When we were really close to finishing up, the production manager called the whole crew from the stage and introduced the entourage to us: "These are the guys that are eating all of your food." I have to take my hat off to that production manager. That took some balls, as that tour was all about kissing butt and politics for him. He didn't get fired for that, but he did get fired later on for something just as stupid, if not more stupid.

It may have been in Indianapolis, at the Convention Center. Anyway, we were playing a ballroom in some small room, and the ceiling was about eighteen feet from the deck of the stage. R. Kelly had this backdrop that was a picture of the skyline of Chicago. It was really important that we hang it every day. Well, the buildings on the backdrop started at about thirty feet from the bottom of the drop, and about fifteen feet above that was nothing but black sky. When we hung it, all you could see was the sky behind the set. When the production manager saw it, he told us to take it down because the drop would get destroyed lying all over the ground. So we did. Well, right before the show, someone had a fit that the drop was not up, and we scrambled to get it up. Nothing had changed, you only saw sky from the audience, but that made them happy. The production manager got fired that night. The rumor was that it was the backdrop incident, but to tell you the truth, with that crowd, it could have been anything.

Right after Chicago we headed to Jackson, Mississippi. We had three days off. When we got to the hotel, the Edison Walthall, Tony wandered by the bar and saw they had Johnny Walker blue on the shelf. He ordered one and found it was pretty cheap. I wandered down there and joined him. We ended up pretty drunk and asked the bartender where to get the best steak in town. He told us about this place, but we would have to take a cab to get there. We got a cab and headed out. I wish I could remember the name of that place, because it was amazing. It was in some industrial area with all the warehouses and a small strip mall. Anyway, we ate a great meal. After dinner we hopped in a cab and made a journey to strip bar. This place was great, as well.

It had a whole bunch of different rooms with stages all over the place. Within an hour or so, we were talking with a few girls, drinking with them, and tipping them well. We spent the next few nights in that strip bar (I can't remember its name). The chicks we met were into this really strange music, Type O Negative. It was great music to watch them dance to, but I bought a CD later and could not find a way to like it outside that bar. That was a drunken few nights off, but Tony and I sure had a blast.

Somewhere along the way—I think it was at the Cap Center in Washington D.C., but to tell you the truth I'm not sure where it was—either

Tony or I came upon some acid. We took it right toward the end of the show. Everything was great through load-out, until we could not find the last road case, which held the gel scrollers. Seems something always goes wrong when you decide it is a good idea to trip while working. Just about the time we had finished loading the truck, the acid began to kick in pretty hard. We could not find that road case, but we figured it would show up at some point during load-out and we could put it on another truck. Well, we stacked the scrollers up on the side of the stage and went to locate the missing case. Tony took off one way, and I took off another. I looked all over the backstage area. I could not find it anywhere. I looked and looked for hours, it seemed. The last truck was getting loaded, I had not seen Tony since we split up, and I had not found the case anywhere.

All of a sudden, I see Tony running down the hallway pushing the box. The scroller cases were this dull green color, but this one was dull green plus streaks of white on the sides. As he got closer, I saw that the white was frosting all over the case. He got it on the rigging truck and sat down on a chair, breathing really heavily. I asked him what happened and he labored through the whole explanation. He said he was up a few levels up in the arena, tripping really hard and feeling quite lost. He saw a room with a light on and wandered in. What he found was the end of a birthday party or something. There was a cake, and he noticed it was on our road case. He got the cake off and spent a great while trying to find his way back to the loading dock. What a nightmare! At least we found the case and didn't have to explain that to the shop.

We played Little Rock on that run, and I saw Connie. The end of the tour was down in Florida. We played the Sun Dome, my old stomping grounds. My friend was still the production manager there, and he loaned me his car after we loaded in. Tony had never been to the Mons Venus, so I just had to get him there. We went in the afternoon and made it back by the show. I think Tony liked that little excursion. The Mons was still like it was in the old days. The laws were a lot more lax back then.

We finished that tour in Jacksonville at the Veteran's Memorial Coliseum on June 9, 1996. It could not have come soon enough, as far as I was concerned. I was tired of all the drama, but I made it through. With all of the drinking that Tony and I did, I should have checked into rehab when I got home, but that was not the case.

FURTHUR FESTIVAL 1996

I went right back to the shop and started working on the Furthur Festival, which was Metropolitan Entertainment's answer to the death of Jerry Garcia. To tell the truth, it was a great idea, and it lasted for three summers after that. The following of the Grateful Dead had grown to enormous numbers. So many people followed the Grateful Dead all summer long, there needed to be something for them. This run was awesome; it was a touring festival like Lollapalooza, with ten bands on stage throughout the day—Hot Tuna, John Wesley Harding, Los Lobos, The Flying Karamazov Brothers, Bruce Hornsby, Alvin Youngblood Hart, Mickey Hart's Mystery Box, and Ratdog made up the line-up.

Not only did I start working on it, I was told that I had been chosen to be the crew chief of the lighting crew. I never expected that, but it sure was cool. The only bad part was that now I was going to have to find out why all of my other crew chiefs did things the way that they did and not how I thought they should be done. My first task was to find a way to make friends with a guy named RT, whom I had basically just ignored for two years on the Grateful Dead.

We built the rig in LA at the shop and headed to Rome, Georgia, for rehearsals on June 15, 1996. The hotel was about thirty minutes from the arena that we worked at, so we had a bunch of time to gel as a crew on the ride every day. The cool part was that now I had to drive, being the crew chief and all. I finally got my driving privileges back! We set the rig up pretty quickly and got going on rehearsals that evening. Jay was programming for Candice all night, as had always been the case. The second day of rehearsals, I sat down with the sound crew chief, Mark, and we talked about how we had to change all the Grateful Dead rules out here to make this thing work like a real tour. We knew it would not be that hard, now that the Grateful Dead backline guys were not out with us. The issue was going to be RT. That night we sat down with RT to discuss what we thought we should do.

To our surprise, RT, the stage manager, was open to anything and everything we had to suggest. I guess he was worried about the overnight shows and three-in-a-rows. We didn't do that on the Grateful Dead, and I think he saw it as a huge hurdle for himself. At this realization, Mark and I figured we would just go for it. We told him that within a week we could get this show out, with the last truck door shutting within two hours. He said there was no way, but he would try things our way, to see. When we finished talking with RT, Mark and I decided we should probably push the envelope pretty hard in the beginning, just to see how far we could go.

On the last day of rehearsals, everyone is always trying to get out at a decent time to get a little rest before the tour ramps up. We were supposed to start loading out around nine p.m. Mr. Hart was still playing away with his band. As was the case with the Grateful Dead, there were no lights hanging over the band. All of the lights were on the perimeter of where the bands actually played, so I started to bring down the trusses. I went over to RT and asked him if that was cool. He told me to go ahead and see what happened. I did, and before Mr. Hart was done playing, we had all of the trusses down and out of the way, one at a time. I don't even think Mr. Hart knew we were working all around him. If he did, he never even flinched.

That was the first time, I believe, in a long time that any work was done on stage before the backline was packed, and probably the first time work was done while the band was playing. That set the tone for the whole run. With that being the case, Mark and I got together and started to find ways to work quickly. This was the beginning of the Furthur Festival turning into a real tour, with its own rules, instead of the old Grateful Dead way. (We would also find, a few years later, that the band was never the reason that certain rules existed on the Grateful Dead. We started to realize that there were a whole lot of other people that needed control over other people and departments.)

We packed up in Rome and headed to Atlanta to kick off the tour. We played the Lakewood Amphitheatre on June 19, 1996. The crowd was there, and the Grateful Dead atmosphere began to fill the air. It was like that all summer long. We did all of the amphitheaters down the East Coast: Blockbuster in Charlotte, Walnut Creek in Raleigh, Virginia Beach, and Nissan in Bristow. The next show was to be in Noblesville, IN. Deer Creek Music Center (home of the famous acid trip).

Deer Creek is a really small place. There is not much room for moving equipment around. They have made the loading dock bigger in recent times, but back then it was really tight. We had a day off on the front end, so production decided to have a meeting at the venue so we could all sit and discuss how we might deal with ten bands moving on and off the whole stage. By that point, we had loaded out in our two-hour goal that we had set, and knew that this would not be the case here. We all sat in an office and hashed out ways to make this work. By the time we were done, we had a really good plan, and the next day went a lot smoother than it would have.

From there we headed to Alpine Valley, in East Troy, WI, the place where we lost Stevie Ray Vaughan. That thought always puts a damper on the day. We did Chicago, The World (a huge shed just outside of Chicago), Cuyahoga Falls, Blossom Music Center, Clarkston, Pine Knob, Darien Lake, Saratoga Performing Arts Center, Hartford, The Meadows, Old Orchard Beach, Mansfield, and Great Woods, and then on July 11, 1996, we played Liberty State Park, NJ. That was a treat.

We pulled up in the buses, and the first sight I had that morning was of The Statue of Liberty. That park is not a normal stop on any tour, but I sure am glad that it was a stop for us. There was a stage built, and the whole backdrop for the day was NYC and the Statue. I can't think of a nicer way to spend a day! From there we headed to Camden, NJ (The Entertainment Center), Burgettstown, PA (Star Lake), Columbus, OH (Polaris), and then to my favorite: St. Louis, and a day off!

I slept in that day to rest for a trip over the *Escape from New York* bridge that night. There were a few of us on that trip to East Brooklyn, IL. Roxy's was the first stop. Somebody had put some work into Roxy's, because it was much better lit and the atmosphere was completely different. Unlike the times I was there before, it was packed. We got bored after a while and headed on our way to PT's across the street. PT's is a fancy place, and we are all just roadies, so there is always a little controversy in that scene. We sat down at a stage and watched this girl dance. She did her two songs, and when I went to give her a tip, she just grabbed it out of my hand and started talking to some other guy about ten feet away. I know, no big deal, but I tipped her and I wanted to see her dance. I was pretty drunk and started to make a fuss. Before long there was a bouncer in my face, and I calmly told him I wanted to see her dance or I wanted my money back. Well, that scene went on for a bit of time, and the stripper got pretty mad. Finally the bouncer said, "I will get your dollar back but you guys have to leave now." I said OK, and I figured at this point we were going to walk out the door into a police car. He made her give me the dollar and escorted us out. No cops. We decided to head to another strip bar across the street.

As soon as we got close to the door, the bouncer told us to keep walking. The word was out, so I guess we could not go into any more strip bars that night. We ended up getting a cab and heading back to the Double Tree in Maryland Heights. To this day, I do not know how I got that tip back; it really surprised me and the guys I was with. I guess a story can lessen the damper of cutting the night short.

From St. Louis we headed west to Kansas City (Sandstone Amphitheater), Denver (Fiddler's Green), then a day off in Park City. We played Wolf Mountain in Park City, the Hilton in Reno, then the Gorge in George, Washington. On July 27 we played Eugene, Oregon. We played at the Country Fairgrounds. It was a little stage, and we didn't hang any of our lights that day. It was the home of Ken Kesey, author of "One Flew Over The Cookoo's Nest." This was a show to remember for all of the hippies. The original Further Bus was housed there. It was in the back of the venue all day. When we arrived that morning, there was no real building in which catering was set up. Rather, we were escorted into an old hippie commune, and we had an amazing organic meal. The people there were amazing, so loving and special.

Jay had rented a van the day before, and he had a friend that lived about forty-five minutes up the river. Since we didn't hang our lights that day, the lighting crew planned to head out to Jay's friend's house for some fishing and an evening crawfish boil. We were a little late getting on our way due to the fact that no one wanted to leave—Ken Kesey and Wavy Gravy had taken the stage to open the show. It was pretty early in the day and those two had apparently eaten some acid sometime before, because whatever they were laughing and talking about made no sense at all. We all, including the audience, just stared in amazement as the silliness on stage erupted. When someone finally talked them off of the stage, we got in the van and headed out.

The day was amazing. We fished in a pond most of the afternoon, then hopped in the stream and caught crawfish. That evening we sat under what seemed like a million stars and ate crawfish for hours. We made it back to Eugene just before the show ended, hopped on the bus, and headed to Sacramento. We played Cal Expo, then Shoreline in San Francisco, and then we had a day off in Ventura, CA.

It was nice walking home to my place in Ventura. I dropped off most of my stuff at my house. We played the Ventura Fairgrounds August 1, then Irvine Meadows the next day. The final show was in Phoenix, at the Desert Sky Pavilion, on August 4. We had a day off the day before, and they put us in this grand resort called the Wigwam Resort. It was a pretty amazing place. When we got there, we were given invitations to an end-of-the-tour party. Production put on an amazing event under the stars. The food, drink, and company will never be beat.

SANTANA 1996

When I got back to the shop, I was told that I would be doing Santana. It started in Reno on September 6, 1996.

The lighting crew was just two of us: David and I. David was the guy from the Primus tour that we let sleep in when we were in Charlotte. We unloaded the gear, which was in shambles, set it all up, and found that half of the snake was built wrong. The snake is the 330 foot cable that runs from the dimmers to the front of house console. It is one of the main ingredients for running the lighting show. Some of the cables were taped in backwards. As we were fixing the snake, I noticed that one of the three trucks which were unloaded that morning was driving away. I went to the production office and asked where that truck was going and was told that this was a two-truck tour; the third truck was just transport to the first show. I said there was no way I was going to fit in three-fourths of a truck. I was told that I would have to find a way.

When we got the snake fixed, David and I found out that most of the moving lights had major problems. We started to work on them, but there was no way that we would be ready for the show that night. The lighting designer was furious! David and I just worked and worked until show time, but never got the rig in any kind of acceptable form. We did a horrible show, then tore everything down and tried to fit it in the two trucks. As you can imagine, it didn't fit. We had lighting gear stacked to the ceiling all the way to the back of the truck. The stuff that would not fit filled up the bays in the bus. We took an ear-load of yelling the whole time. When we got to the Santa Barbara Bowl the next morning, the stagehands went nuts when they saw the Icon console perched at the ceiling of the truck. Somehow we got it all down and out, but to tell you the truth I'm not sure how nothing got broken and no one got hurt.

The lights still didn't work, and I still had to figure out how to re-pack everything to make it fit in the truck. The only saving grace was that we had two shows in Santa Barbara, so we could stay all night to fix the broken lights and figure out a packing plan. David and the LD programmed all night, so it was basically up to me to sort through the mess. The first show was crappy, but before the night was over, we had gotten the whole lighting rig working. I sat up the rest of the night figuring out the pack plan and had a truck from LSD come the next day to take away the boxes I needed to empty in order for everything to fit. I had drawn pictures of the truck pack and had about two inches to spare in the drawings. That night loading the truck was a nightmare. It fit, and there were two inches to spare, but I sure did learn a few more lessons in being a crew chief. I now had more questions that I knew had to be asked before you start a tour. The big one is "How many trucks do we have for lighting?"

We played Cuthbert Amphitheatre in Eugene, the Puyallup Fair in Washington, Concord Pavilion in California, Tulare County Fair, Shoreline Amphitheatre, San Diego's Hospitality Point, and then The Greek Theatre in LA. We did three shows there, September 20-22. We stayed at the Hyatt on Sunset, aka the Riot House. The Riot House has stories dating back to the '60s. Keith Richards threw a TV out a window, Jim Morrison was said to have been dangling off the balcony, and motorcycles have ridden down the hallways. It is not the most beautiful of hotels, but it sure has some history. Apparently, we were to make some history on that Sunday, September 22.

No one has ever gotten to the bottom of the story, but at some point during football that morning, there was a call to the hotel that plastic bags of water were being dropped from one of the balconies of the hotel onto the sidewalk on the strip. The room that the caller described was where two sound guys were watching the game. There came a knock at their door, and after loads of arguments they were thrown out of the hotel. No one was hurt by the falling bags of water, but that didn't seem to matter; the two sound guys had to leave. They were, however, able to stay on the bus until we left later that day for the show. The hotel management told them that if they were seen outside of that bus, they would be turned over to the police. The only problem with that was that the buses used to park under an overhang to the west of the hotel, and they got no reception on the TV. I'm sure those two will deny any part of that today, just as they did that day.

From LA, we headed east. We played San Bernardino (Blockbuster Pavilion), Phoenix (Compton Terrace—a very famous yet weird venue), Tucson (Pima County Fair), Albuquerque (Tingley Coliseum), El Paso (UTEP), Dallas (Starplex Amphitheater), and then San Antonio, Texas (Sunken Gardens). We had a day off on October 2, then two shows, October 3 and 4, at Sunken Gardens. We stayed at La Mansion Del Rio, right on the river. That is one of the most beautiful hotels I have ever stayed at. The Spanish feel is amazing and the rooms are wonderful. That night, David and I found our way to a pub on the river and had a few Guinnesses and a meal before we crashed out.

When we loaded in the next day, there was this beautiful chick that was in charge of the roofing system over the stage. I fell in love the moment I saw her. She was just a natural beauty. She had really long brownish-blonde hair, dressed like an outdoors girl, and had these hiking boots on. I had a hard time keeping my mind on work all day. By the end of the day we had spoken a few times, and I asked her if she wanted to grab a beer on the river that night. We didn't have to be back at the venue until after lunch the next day, so there was no need to get up early. She said she would meet me at the hotel after the show, and I gave her my room number and told her to call up. I went back to the hotel, and as soon as I was out of the shower the phone rang. It was she. I got ready quickly, and we went to the pub. We had a few beers, and then the bar closed so we headed back down the river. We sat outside the hotel on a bench and talked for a good while, then we ended up in my room. That night was one of those dream nights. Everything was perfect.

The next morning, we woke up under all of those plush covers holding each other. She got up and took a shower. I hopped in after her, and when I got out, she was sitting in a robe at the desk in the room. She asked me to sit down, so I did, across the desk from her. It was a little tense as she began to speak. She told me that her boyfriend, who she had not mentioned the day or evening before, was on the crew. I told her I would be cool, but that I really liked her. She said she liked me too, and that she was not going to be with him much longer anyway. With that we crawled back in bed and just laid there for a few hours. Then she got up and left to get ready for work.

I felt a bit bad when I got to work. I didn't meet her boyfriend until much later that day, but when I did I just felt horrible. Jan and I kept in touch for several years after that. We wrote letters, and I always called when I was near San Antonio, but she was always working somewhere else when I was in town. In the end, I got a letter from her when I was living in Calabassas. She wrote that she still missed me, even though it was only letters and phone calls, but seeing as that would be the case, it seemed, for a long time, she had met another guy and wanted to get married and have kids. What was I supposed to say to that? I could not have kids while I was on the road, so I told her that it was cool and that I would love to find a way to come steal her away, but that would never happen. I wished her well, as I am wishing her well now, as I write. I hope she has everything she wants. I wish I could have been a part of it, but living on the road has its drawbacks. Love is the biggest drawback of them all!

From San Antonio we headed to Houston's Cynthia Mitchell Pavilion and then Tampa's Sun Dome, my old stomping grounds. When we got to Tampa, I saw my family for a while that evening. It was nice working at the Sun Dome with all my old friends. My sister brought Chloe, her daughter, and there is still a picture floating around of her with a Santana sign in the background. From Tampa we headed to the Orlando Arena, then to Sunrise, Florida, and the Sunrise Musical Theatre. We played two shows there, October 11 and 12. After load-out (and a few at the bar) on the twelfth, I was heading back to my room at the Sunrise Hilton when the elevator door opened. To my surprise, coming out was Bob Weir. I would have just shaken my head and gone about my business, but he stopped and said, "What are you doing here? I haven't seen you around lately, don't you work with us?" I said I did the last two years of the Grateful Dead and then this last Furthur festival, but I was now working for Santana. We ended up talking for a long time in the hallway outside of the elevator. I can't even remember what we were talking about, but it seemed to last a lifetime. It was very surreal. Toward the end of the conversation, I told him I had an early flight to NYC and needed to get going. He said goodbye and we said we hoped to see each other next summer. I did the Furthur Festival the next summer, but we never spoke again. I swear this business has the weirdest moments pop up at the weirdest times.

We flew to NY and checked into the Warwick Hotel on Fifty-Fourth. David called me and wanted to know if I knew where to get filthy porn movies. He said they were not for him, but an old roommate from college was into midgets and he wanted to find some movies for him. I told him I knew a place and would meet him down in the lobby in a few. Back then, Forty-Second Street was not Disney yet, and there were tons of shady places all over the place. We headed down there and ended up in this video place on Ninth Ave. David found everything he could imagine in there. I have no idea what he bought, but we spent about an hour in there looking. When we left, David wanted to see if the Rangers were playing that night, so we looked at a newspaper and saw that they were. David is a huge hockey fan, which was quite the eye opener when I found out he grew up in Hawaii. The Rangers were playing Calgary that night, so we walked down Ninth Ave then cut over to MSG to see if we could get some tickets.

When we got to the box office there was a line. When we got to the window, the only seats that they had left were "obstructed view" at the top of the arena and seats right behind the Rangers' bench. Well, $125 later, we had awesome seats for a game that I liked but didn't know any of the rules. That was my first hockey game ever, and I have been hooked ever since. That game was awesome. We had a blast, and to add to all of the excitement, the Rangers won and both Wayne Gretzky and Mark Messier had goals. How is that for a first hockey game?

We did two shows at the Beacon Theatre, October 15 and 16. Otmar Liebert had been opening up the whole tour, but in NYC Vernon Reid opened both nights. After a huge sandwich from the Carnegie Deli, I did the last show of the tour and packed the truck for the last time. The next day I flew back to LA and got my next tour, which was The Counting Crows.

COUNTING CROWS

It's hard to begin this one. This was to be the worst experience to date. That was the way it felt at the time, at least, but looking back, it was one of the best learning experiences I had. I learned about young bands, breaking into the theater scene, co-workers and their relationships with LSD, and a band's entourage hired as help. The whole run was hard on many levels, and it took all I could muster to make it as long as I did.

We began with rehearsals in New Haven, CT, at the Palace Theatre, but the worst part was before the tour. I was trying to put together the system in the shop a few weeks before. Henry, the lighting designer, was an old LSD tech. He was great at fixing color changers and was one of the best crew chiefs that LSD had. I thought I was in pretty good hands with him, but as time passed I found he was pretty nervous and this was his first LD job. I asked all the questions that I needed to ask, but in his nervousness he didn't give me all the right answers.

The whole system was built, but Henry had a color changer on every single light in the rig. Not so bad in terms of color changers today, but back then the LSD color changers had controllers that only ran thirty-two changers. You could make groups with the controller and run more than thirty-two, but basically if you wanted control of all changers by themselves, you had to wire the rig with a certain amount of controllers running a certain amount of changers. If you sent information from two controllers at the same time to a single power supply, you would blow up the system.

I spoke with Henry, and he said he was good with groups and that I would be able to get away with two controllers. When I got to New Haven, Paul (the dimmer guy) and I put up the rig and got everything working during the first day. That night as we sat down to program the lighting system for the show, Henry gave me the news that he needed control of every changer individually. Well, that threw a wrench in everything, and I ended up on the phone with the shop for about thirty minutes trying to figure out how to fix the wiring so that I could accomplish that task. The only answer from the shop was to bring down the whole rig and re-wire everything.

I gave this info to Henry and Paul, and Henry about went through the ceiling. He would loose about two hours or more of programming if we did that. I had no idea what to do. I started to ask Henry, knowing he was a great color-changer tech, but he replied with "I'm the LD, you are the crew chief. Fix it now and fast." So in all of my stupidity I decided to y-split two controllers and fix the problem. That was the only thing that the shop told me never to do, but it was fast and, to my surprise, it worked and we got back to work in about twenty minutes.

When the shop explained that I would blow up the system, they also explained why that would happen. If you sent a cue from two different controllers at the same time, that would overload the power supplies and blow up the whole rig. I figured that as long as I sent the cues at different times, everything would be fine.

In the end, it was fine. I ran the controllers in the show, and there were only cue changes between songs, so I could delay the cues long enough to stop the overloading of the power supplies. I left things the way they were and just never sent two cues at once.

Anyway, after we got that all sorted out, we finished programming over the next two nights, and started the tour on November 12, 1996. The best part of the few nights in New Haven was when I found out that we were sharing rooms. That was a first for me, but it was the norm several years before. I shared a room with Paul, and that got to be quite the pain as time went on.

From New Haven we headed to Boston and we had a day off. The whole technical crew met that evening in the lobby of the Tremont Hotel, and started what would become a reoccurring act of drunken, coked-up partying throughout the whole tour. We ended up stumbling home from the Glass

Slipper at some ungodly hour. The next day we played the Orpheum. By that time, I had figured out that Paul was only going to do dimmers; I would have to build the whole rig alone. It was not that big, and I was able to do it, but when Paul announced to me that he was hired to do dimmers and that was all he would do, I started to get pissed off. I let it build inside the whole tour, and it really sucked for me. I also found out that he didn't want to have anything to do with the opening act, Cake, so I had to run that as well.

We played two nights in Boston and then headed to Ottawa. The show in Ottawa was not until November 18, so after the long ride on the bus, Paul and I headed across the street from the Delta Ottawa hotel to a hockey bar and drank "Blue" and watched hockey until we stumbled back to the hotel that night. We played the National Arts Centre. From Ottawa we headed to Montreal and played the St. Denis Theatre. From there we went to Quebec City and played the Capitol Theatre. I think that may have been the coldest night I have ever experienced. When we loaded the trucks after the show, the wind was howling. It was so cold that no one wanted to go out there. When we finally finished, I thought I would die.

From Quebec City, we headed to Toronto for a day off, and Paul and I ended up in another hockey bar getting smashed. We played Massey Hall for two nights, November 22 and 23. From Toronto we went to Pittsburgh and played the Palumbo Center the next night. From there we went to Washington, D.C., for a day off at the Morrison Clark Hotel.

On November 26, we played the 9:30 Club. Up to this day, Henry would have me in the venue re-programming all of the color changers from the notes that he had made the night before. I was beat, and sick of working all day long, so that day I told him that we had done nine shows and if he wanted to change anything else, he would be on his own. He told me I had to stay, and I just walked out the door to the bus and went to sleep. I guess that was the best thing to do, because he never asked me to spend the afternoon programming again. We played two nights there and had Thanksgiving the next night in a restaurant in Union Station in DC. I don't think any of the crew ate a thing. Someone ordered a margarita, and from that point on, even as cold and snowy as it was outside, it turned into a Mexican fiesta! By the time we all stumbled to the bus none of us could even talk. We all passed out and headed to New Brunswick, NJ, for a show at the State Theatre on November 29.

On November 30 we checked into The Mayflower Hotel, which used to be on Central Park West. We played the Beacon for two nights and then we had a day off in New York. The second night at the Beacon was one of the worst shows I had ever been a part of. The lighting console was generally set up in the back of the first level. Henry put up a huge fight about not being able to see the lighting system from there, and somehow he made them let us set up next to the sound console in the middle of the house. The placement was just below the balcony, but in front of the edge of it. I had to set up the color changer controllers facing him, so I was basically looking at him with my desks and his console between us. We got the five-minute warning for the show to start, and as I looked at Henry, there was a huge beer falling right between us. It had come from the balcony, and we both saw it at the same moment, about a foot before it slammed onto the lighting console. Needless to say, there would be no proper lights for that show.

As soon as it happened I went flying backstage and told the production manager what had happened, and he said he could hold for fifteen minutes. That was the first time I saw how much Local 1 really does care about everything they do. By the time I had the top off the console, they had a wet-vac and started sucking out the inch of beer that had accumulated in the bottom. We cleaned and dried as much as we could. Even with all of that, the console was shot. When Henry ran the show that night, nothing came up when it was supposed to; there was so much liquid in there that lights just came up randomly every time he touched a fader. About four songs in, I had to just set down my headset; I couldn't take him yelling at me any longer. I'm pretty sure Paul had his off as well, and just the spot operators and Henry were on. I would imagine they had theirs off as well.

That night after the second show was a coke, stripper, and drink-all-you can party. We all went out, and I think we must have hit ten strip bars and snorted more coke than I have ever seen. When we got back to the hotel, at some silly hour, Paul ended up on the phone yelling at his wife for about an hour. That was horrible. I had nowhere to go, so I sat in the hallway and waited. Finally, when he was done, I went back in the room and I passed out. We found out that day that the singer was sick and had lost his voice. We loaded the show out and headed to Philly for two shows at the Tower Theatre. We ended up going back to New York after those Philly shows to make up the two dates. Most of the tech crew flew back to LA after those two shows. The rest of the guys followed a few days later after they played the David Letterman show December 11.

A few days at home was just what I needed. The next shows were not until December 17, at the Wiltern Theater. As much as I like the Le Parc Hotel, sharing a room was out of the question. I needed to get away from Paul, as well as the backline crew chief. The crew chief's name was Six—I know, funny name. I wish he was as funny as his name. Six was a royal pain. He was always fighting with me and moving all of my empty boxes because they were always in his way, he would say. He had been with the band since the beginning, and as the band grew to bigger success, he was nowhere near to a point that he could grow with them. His answer was to yell and show his power all day. Well, his power struggle and fighting would lead to his demise, but not before I took a hit. Anyway, that's later. For the next few days I got to relax.

During that break, I went into the office to talk with my boss about Paul and the fact that he would only do dimmers and that I was doing most of the work alone. My boss just blew up. He said that was not the first time he had heard this about Paul and he would get me someone else. I asked him to let Paul stay out on the tour and to help me find the right words to get him to pitch in a little more, but my boss insisted that Paul be removed. I really didn't want things to go that way, but that was out of my hands now.

On December 17, Paul and I loaded the lighting rig into the Wiltern Theatre in LA. Paul would not even talk to me the whole day, and on top of that Six was being a complete control freak. We did four shows— December 17, 18, 20, and 21. Paul never said a word, and I wanted to rip Six's head off. The only saving grace that week was that the lead singer of the band was dating Courtney Cox at the time, and the cast from "Friends" was there. I didn't really watch that TV show much, but I knew who they were. Actually they were all really nice, and friendly. LA seems to have its own way of trying to make you feel better than you actually do.

I came to find out that my boss told Paul that I didn't like him and that I wanted him replaced with someone that wanted to work. The funny thing about that is that I didn't want anything like that to happen. It didn't matter, though. Paul and my boss were really close, and I was an outsider. Paul thought he should be the crew chief all along, so he resented me. I wish things had turned out different, but as I was to find out in the next few years, I would get caught in several situations that made me almost fail. It is hard to look back and not think that my boss was not out to get me, but I'm not sure that is the case at all. What I realize now is that I needed to learn a few lessons about how and who to trust in this business. Learning lessons like that always suck and are always very hard.

We had a break for Christmas, and we were supposed to meet back up in Houston on January 20 to rehearse before the next leg. I went back to Tampa to spend Christmas with my mom and sister. When I got back to LA I talked with my boss, and he just blew the whole thing off. He asked me if I wanted Jay to take Paul's place, and I agreed. I thought that the whole thing would blow over, but to this day Paul and I have never spoken.

Somewhere in that time, there ended up being a huge split in the crew at LSD. I'm not sure what happened, but everyone was kind of splitting up into two separate groups, and none of those groups intermingled at all.

When we were in the shop rebuilding the show to set back out to Houston, I rebuilt the color mag system properly so I didn't have to play with the timing of the cues anymore. Jay and I also spent a ton of time marking the rig, and by the time we were ready to leave, everything was marked so well that we barely had to tell the stagehands what to do to put the rig up. It was quite a relief having Jay out there, but Six was about to rear his nasty, control freak head. My whole world was about to collapse around me, and I knew it.

We opened that leg at the Houston Music Hall on January 23. The night before, Jay and I went out for a steak. We were told to go to Pappas Bros., and what a choice that was. We sat at the bar and ate one of the best steaks of my life. I had a ribeye that just melted in my mouth. The night after Houston, we played Austin City Coliseum. From Austin we played Dallas (the Dallas Music Complex), then we went on to Tulsa for a day off.

I went to the production manager that day and told him that I could not deal with Six anymore. He was moving my boxes every day and basically driving me mad. The production manager said he was having the same problems with Six on different levels, but with him being so close to the band there was not much he could do at this point. We decided that I would work out where to put my boxes every day before Six got in, and Six

154

could speak with him if he needed anything changed. I told the production manager I didn't want to even speak to Six anymore, and he said not to; I could just come to him when I had an issue and he would deal with Six. The politics were so heavy then, I knew something would blow up before too long.

We played The Brady Theatre in Tulsa on January 27. From Tulsa we went to Oklahoma City and played the Civic Centre Music Hall, then we had a day off, in Fayetteville, AR. Jay and I hung out all day, and we talked a lot about how I should deal with this Six issue. We never came up with anything. Instead we just got drunk and passed out. The next day, January 30, we loaded into Barnhill Arena. The production manager and I sorted my cases out and stacked them way off on the side of the stage. Six showed up and the first thing he did was grab all of the stagehands, un-stacked all of the boxes, and sent them off the stage somewhere in the halls. I walked into the production office and said that they needed to find out where my boxes were going. The production manager blew up. He went straight out to the side of the stage, where Six was working, and laid into him about how he told me where to stack my boxes and they were fine where they were. I was at front of house at this point, which is when Six punched the production manager in the face. As the fight started, Spragettii, the monitor tech, jumped in and broke it up.

Six set up his gear and disappeared until show time. Right before the show, I was called to the office. The production manager sat me down and explained that Six had gone to the tour manager and told him that I was causing every problem on the tour. Since Six had been with the band from the beginning, the production manager could not get the tour manager to listen to anything. I was fired. Somehow, Six punched the production manager and I got fired. Kind of funny! The production manager told me that in the end he agreed to fire me, but if the problems didn't go away, then Six was the next to go.

We did the show that night and headed for Memphis for my last load-in at the Orpheum Theater. Chuck was going to be there to replace me. I showed him the gear and passed it on to him, then we headed to the Rendezvous for some ribs. I left for the airport as soon as we got done eating. I spoke with the salesman of the tour that day, and he told me not to worry. He knew the whole story and I would be fine. He told me there were better ways to go about being stuck in that situation, but he also said he would get me work when I got back.

Jay called me a few weeks later and said that Six was no longer out with them. I guess the problems didn't go away. I found out many years later, when I did a one-off for the band in Tucson, that not only was Six fired but he tried to sue the band for firing him. In the end, they found that he had racked up about $30,000 in credit card bills. (That is what I heard; I don't know how true it was, but it made me feel a little better.) Later that day, I was in the catering room and the tour manager came over and apologized to me for that firing so long ago. I told him it was cool and that I'd started a new gig the next week. It was nice to hear that from him, though.

1997

YANNI, FURTHUR, BRYAN ADAMS, BOWIE

After getting home from the Counting Crows, I was told that I would be replacing a guy on a big Yanni show in China. That ended up being one of the coolest things I would do. We prepped everything in the shop and it got sent over to China. That was the first time I had to deal with any kind of overseas shipments. It was pretty neat to be a part of. Everything had to be counted and written down.

After we packed all of the truck for China, we had a few days at home before flying to Beijing. When we arrived, Serg and I went out for a stroll. We walked all around the hotel area. We ended up in some really strange areas behind some shopping buildings. I'm not sure it was the place for tourists, but it sure was interesting. There were all of these strange rooms made out of wood and tarps, almost like a village of lean–tos. It looked like people were living there, and when I think back now they probably were. What a strange world we had walked into.

As we left that area, Serg saw this bar and said he wanted a beer. The name of the place was Sue's bar. We walked in and there was no one there, just a few women and a bartender. Serg and I walked over to the bar and ordered a beer. As we started to drink, the two girls from the other side of the room headed over and asked us if we wanted to dance. We said no, we just wanted a beer and we would be on our way. They just sat down next to us at the bar and Serg and I started to talk about the strange lean-to place we had wandered into. About halfway through the beers, the two girls asked us about dancing again, and that is when it finally hit us. We were in a bar where you get dates. The girls were hot, but it was pretty strange, and being in Communist China, we just finished our beers and left. As the week passed, we found that there were a lot of those places all around the hotel.

The next day we went into work to start setting up for the show. The show was inside the Forbidden City, which was so cool. There were no trucks to unload, which was strange, but all of the trussing was there. That was it, no lights or dimmers, just truss. We all spread out and started to do our best sign language to get all of the stagehands to start building truss. Chinese and English are nothing alike, so there was absolutely no communication through words. There were a few interpreters, and that helped, but for the most part we all just talked with our hands. About halfway through the day, we broke for lunch. Then we went to the catering building and were fed KFC. We looked at the Chinese guys and they had this amazing Chinese food, which made us a bit jealous. Oh well, we were the guests, and I think they thought we liked "American" food.

After lunch, a few of us were called aside and told that there were some issues at the airport and we would have to go there and explain what some of the gear was so that it would pass through customs. We all hopped in a van and headed to the airport. It took forever, as did traveling anywhere in Beijing. There were four lanes of traffic, but three lanes were taken up by bicycles. I have never in all of my life seen so many people riding bicycles. It was quite a sight. After arriving at the airport, we helped the Chinese guys unpack the gear as it came off of the cargo jet. There was one guy there that was in charge of customs; he would ask the interpreter what the gear was and then decide whether or not we could take it and put it on the trucks for the show.

Well, that turned into a feat in itself. We were told we could not have the lighting consoles, as well as a whole pile of other things that were essential for the show. As he kept saying no, we would stack those things in a pile and move on. We had about seven of these blue stake bed trucks loaded, and a giant pile of gear off to the side that was impounded. Around five p.m. or so, as we were unloading the cargo and placing it on the blue trucks, no one was asking any more questions about gear, it was just coming off the pallets and onto the trucks. When we finally got to the end of the gear, we asked the interpreter about the stuff in the pile off to the side, and she said to just put it on a truck and they would come down and take it back if they really wanted it. We asked if we would get in trouble, and she said that the customs guy's job was from nine a.m. to five p.m. He was at home now and could care less what happened when he was not there. How strange!

The next day we showed up at the Forbidden City to find all of our gear unloaded and sitting on the sidewalk outside of the walls. It seems that all deliveries in Beijing happen at night. There are little blue trucks buzzing around the city delivering goods. Nothing is delivered during the day. That would come to haunt me in the end, but it was pretty cool then. We got to work and started setting everything up. It was a great day, until lunch rolled around and we got fed McDonald's. That was the last day of that, though; someone asked if we could get the Chinese food like the locals, so that was what we got for the next few days.

We finished loading everything in and began the process of programming. We had some free time then, and all of us were heading out at night and drinking. One night we went to the Hard Rock, which was a blast, until one of the guys left with one of the interpreters. They got about two blocks away and got pulled over by about six police cars. We found out the next day that the police thought she was Chinese and he was not allowed to be leaving with her. Turns out she was not from China and had all of the papers to prove it. The police let them go, but we all got a great lesson in what was OK and not OK there really quickly. Seems the date bars are the only place that you can hook up with a girl. (In the end, the guy that got pulled over kept in touch with that girl and they are married now.)

For the next few days, we worked and went out to eat for lunch. We would walk across Tiananmen Square to the far end where there were a ton of cool places to eat. The day that I paid, we ate at this place that served soup and sandwiches. I still have no idea what kind of meat I ate that day, but I would eat it again. When the bill came, I paid the equivalent of fifty cents American. Can't beat that for three delicious meals. The walk across the square every day was weird. You could only imagine what went on there, and how scary it was.

When we finally did the show, everything went great. They made a video of it, and we all got our names in magazines. It truly was one of the coolest places to go. Everything was so different from anything that we grew up with here in America. After we loaded out, I had to fly straight back to LA and go to work putting the Further Festival together.

I was a mess. I literally flew straight back to LA and went to work. The jet lag was horrendous. Somehow I pulled it together and got everything in place for the tour. It was the same crew as the year before, except Jay had quit touring and moved to Hawaii. Frank was going to be the operator for the tour. I was a little nervous, as he had been my crew chief for two years on the Dead. Now I was his crew chief. Things worked out well in the end.

Every morning I would get my stagehands and I would send all of the girls to work with Frank setting up the console and running the snakes. He was in heaven. It took him a few days to figure out what I was doing, but when he did he laughed and liked it.

Frank used to pull this trick on me about once a week. After he was done working he would go to the bus. I had about an hour of work still before I was done, so Frank would call me on the radio and tell me he had a problem with the show and needed to talk to me right then. I would have to leave the stage and head out to the bus. When I would enter the back lounge, he would have a line the size of my thumb laid out on the table and would tell me, "Good job," and make me snort the massive line of coke. After a while it was funny, but the first few times that I left and had to go load two trucks it sucked. I could not even get a single word out of my mouth. The loaders hated me.

That tour turned into a blast. We all got to see each other every summer, and we all looked forward to it. One of the highlights was The Black Crowes. They were great day in and day out. A few people would not return, but for the most part the core was always the same. By the end of that run, Frank had told me that I was really good as a crew chief. I don't know if he ever knew how much that meant to me. Maybe he does now.

Before I had even gotten home I was informed that I would be going out on Bryan Adams as the crew chief. Wow. All of a sudden I was the crew chief for a tour that I was just a truss builder for a few years before. There were a lot of bad things about that tour, but in the end I began to understand a lot more about touring and trusting. By then I was not smoking pot anymore. That would be the biggest problem for me, as it turned out.

The lighting designer had made sure that he brought his pot-smoking buddies over from England to keep him company on the American leg. I wish he had brought a crew chief as well. Instead I became the kicking post (literally) for his power tantrums. I think that may have been the hardest three weeks of my life. I was pretty serious about keeping the whole rig working, but the rest of the crew was so high they never could even get everything plugged in properly. I lost fifteen pounds in the first week and a half, climbing around and plugging everything in that was left unplugged in the morning. Luckily the tour was only three weeks long. At one point I was almost fired, as along with the whole lighting company, for things that were completely out of my control. That tour ended on September 2, and not a bit too soon. I flew home from Nashville and had one day at home before I headed out to do David Bowie.

I flew out of LA September 4 to Vancouver, BC, to start the tour. The LD was a hard guy to work for. His name was Jerry, and he had a reputation of flying off the handle. I found that he and I worked well together, though. Everyone else had worked with him before and didn't really seem to get along with him. I just did my normal thing of just trying to get everything to work every day and to make the LD happy. The stage manager, Jim, didn't like that at all. We did the Plaza of Nations in Vancouver, the Paramount Theatre in Seattle, and then had a day off in San Francisco. Only two shows in, I knew I was going to have a problem with Jim.

This tour was really cool, though. It was Bowie playing all theaters and clubs. The problem ended up being that I wanted to put the whole rig up every day, to keep Jerry happy, and Jim wanted me to cut the rig (use only part of it) regularly so he could have the stage quicker. We butted heads those first two shows, then in San Francisco, after the show at the Warfield, I went to take a shower and Jim said "No time for that, get on the bus." I said I was taking a shower and he could leave me behind if he wanted to. That sent him in a spin.

The next day we were in the Hollywood Athletic Club, and it was a silly little place to fit the rig. Jim was all over me to cut down the rig, and I was working with the rigger, Gommie, to find a way to fit it. Jim started to yell at me and I just walked away. After we got everything set up, my pager went off: it was the shop. I spoke with my boss and he said I had to find a way to get along with Jim, there was no one to replace me.

I headed up to the production office where Chuck (the production manager) and Jim were working out some labor issues. I waited till I had the chance, then I asked Jim why he had called my boss without trying to sort through the issues with me first. Chuck told us that no one was getting fired and that we had to work it out. Jim and I headed down stairs, and before long we were at each other again. I told him to hit me if that would help. Something made him stop. He just walked away. We never really had a problem after that. I was sure I was heading home, like back on the Counting Crows tour, but not this time.

I'm glad I was till out there. We had a blast, and to see Bowie in all those small venues was awesome. We played the Vic Theatre in Chicago, Metropolis in Montreal, The Warehouse in Toronto, Orpheum in Boston, Electric Factory in Philly, The Chili Pepper in Ft. Lauderdale, The Supper club in NYC, and then Radio City Music Hall. There were more places, but, all in all, it was just awesome. After the run through the States and Canada, we played one show in Mexico City at the Foro Sol. It was a huge stadium. Quite a difference from the venues we'd been in, but to tell you the truth, Mr. Bowie had the crowd in his hands whether we were in a five-hundred-seat club or that huge stadium. We ended that tour on October 24, 1997. I flew back to LA from Mexico City.

I was home for a couple of days and then joined back up with the Bowie crew for a tour of South America. I went to LAX and met the video guy, Rick. We checked in together, as everyone else was coming in from somewhere else. When we got to the gate, there was almost no one there. We also realized that we had business class tickets. That was a first for both of us. I guess in the deal that production has with Bowie, on all overseas flights the crew flies business class. About fifteen minutes before we boarded, they called Rick and I up front and handed us new tickets. The flight was overbooked and they put us in first class. WOW. That may be the only word to describe first class on a 747! We were flying with kings and queens up there. If I had the money to fly like that every day I would. It was unbelievable!

This was a short tour, a week and a half total, but being in South America it ended up being one long day with little naps. We had done a lot of coke on the run through the States, but in South America it was the only thing on the menu for breakfast, lunch, and dinner. It was the good stuff to, the stuff I grew up doing in Florida. There were no hard crashes at the end, and you didn't want to do another line every ten minutes. I wish the coke was still that good in the States. I would still be doing it. We played Curitiba, Brazil first. That was where Chuck was from. Being in South America was cool, but it was even cooler when the production manager was a native who was treated like a king. We all were! We played the Predriera Paula Leninski. It was really cool. There was a pond in the back of the house. I have a picture somewhere from there.

After Curitiba we played the Estadio Do Ibirapuera in Sao Paulo, which is an old stadium in the middle of town. The crowds down there were awesome. The amount of work we did in the amount of time was dreadful, though. From Sao Paulo, we went to Rio De Janiero. We got in first thing in the morning and checked into the Intercontinental Hotel. We left straight away for a show that night at the Metropolitan, which was a venue under a mall. Some of the guys went shopping, but I just remember doing some coke and then passing out on the side of the stage after we were set up. (That was the good stuff, remember? You could enjoy your buzz and still fall asleep.) When I woke up, Mr. Bowie was there for sound check and his wife, Iman, was on the side of the stage. If you think she is pretty in pictures, you should see her in person! Just a beautiful woman!

We got back to the hotel late that night, and when I walked into my room I went straight to the balcony and fired up a smoke. The sound of the ocean was awesome. I sat and finished my cig and decided to sleep out there. I grabbed all of the sheets off the bed and crashed to the sound of the waves in Rio!

The next day we were on a flight to Santiago, Chile. I crashed most of the way, but woke up at the perfect time. I saw the Andes in the distance. Those mountains were popping out of the clouds like diamonds in sand! They were huge! Before long we headed into the clouds and everything was white. About five minutes later, as we dropped out of the clouds, I was as scared as I had ever been in my life. We were in a quaint valley between two huge rock cliffs. I looked out both sides of the airplane and it seemed as if the wings would swipe a rock at any point. I don't ever think I will forget that sight, but the best sight was still to come that day.

We checked into the Sheraton San Cristobal. I was beat, and as soon as I hit the bed I was out. When I woke up a few hours later, I walked over to the window. I was up about nineteen floors or so, and the window ran from the ceiling to the floor. I was looking out over the city when all of a sudden everything started to shake. Earthquake, and I had nowhere to go. As I stood at the window, the building started to bend forward. I was leaning back as far as I could, but I just couldn't move. As I stood there not moving, I could see into the room below me. The building had literally bent so far, I was looking down instead of out. To this day, I don't get very close to any windows in tall buildings.

In Santiago, we played at the Court Central-Estadio Nacional. It was this tennis court that was sunk right down in the ground from street level. Everything got dumped off the truck and had to go down in this hole. It was quite a pain. Getting all of that stuff back up was worse. Anyway, it happened and the show was great.

We flew to Buenos Aires the next day and loaded into the Ferrocalli Oeste Stadium the next day. That place was huge. We were playing a festival show, and we had hung our rig among and within the festival rig. For the bands before us, our lighting trusses were flown up higher than the rest of the lights so that they would not get in the way. We also had a few lights on the front truss that needed to get pointed at key positions on the stage, so I had to go up right before we played and focus those lights. That is when I found out what happens when the South American rig is not grounded and ours is.

In order to reach the truss, I had to climb up the steel and mount a different truss. Then I had to jump from truss to truss until I got to the one I needed to get to. Well, as I reached out from one of our trusses to get on one of theirs, all of the sudden I was grounding the South American rig and got shocked. Luckily I noticed right away and let go. I proceeded to climb up one of the chain motors to the roof and scurry through the roof to where I needed to be. I slid down the chain to that truss and pointed all of the lights. The guys down below were supposed to bring me back up so that I could get back into the ceiling, but the band came right out on stage and I was stuck. It took about half the show to get back up that chain and through the roof with a rock show going on.

That was not the first time I did something stupid in the name of Rock and Roll, and it would not be the last. Everyone back in those days did dumb things. We just did them, and no one thought any different.

That was the last show of the tour, and that would be the last time I worked for Mr. Bowie. It was a wonderful time. No Doubt was opening up for us on most of that tour. (And yes, we all had and probably still do have crushes on Gwen Stefani.) As we got on the plane the next day, our seats were up in the top of the 747. After I sat, I noticed that No Doubt was coming up the stairs to sit up there with us. I had an empty seat next to me, and, sure enough, there she sat! I was out of my mind. It took almost the whole flight before I could even say hello, but after I did, we talked about Los Feliz (an area in LA). I was dating a girl that lived there at the time, so we talked for a bit about the Dresden Room and a few sushi bars. At one point Gwen told me she wanted to buy a house there. I don't know if she ever did, but I was sure happy that I finally got "hello" out of my mouth. She was wonderful to speak with. I got off the plane in LA and we all went our separate ways.

1998

CLAPTON, FURTHER,LOVE, DEEP PURPLE, FAMILY VALUES, KORN

Eric Clapton started with a flight to Minneapolis on March 3, 1998. What a show! What a man! To this day, I still think about "Sunshine of Your Love"! I have been blessed with seeing some of the most amazing artists on this planet. I guess that is why I started all of this so long ago. I loved and still love Rock and Roll. I got lucky, but I also followed what I loved.

The first leg of Clapton ran till April 26. We went from Minneapolis to Kansas City, St. Louis, Moline, Milwaukee, Detroit, Chicago, Cleveland, Boston, Philly, Washington, NYC, Charlotte, Knoxville, Tampa, and Miami. Three of the lighting crew were from Ireland, and two of us were from LA. We had a great time. As always there were a few issues between the European lighting guys and us, but in the end, we have always worked for an English lighting company, so you just work your way through it.

We flew home for a few days, then we all met back up in Pittsburgh on May 10, 1998. The second leg ran through Cincinnati, Chapel Hill, Nashville, Memphis, Houston, New Orleans, Dallas, San Antonio, Phoenix, San Diego, LA, Anaheim, Las Vegas, San Jose, Sacramento, Boise, Portland, and Seattle.

We had a day off in Chapel Hill, and the rigger for the crew was from there. He invited all of us to go on his boat and go water skiing. There were about ten of us that went. We had a blast. The European guys were in heaven. They skied all day. I grew up doing that, so I waited until the last part of the day and hopped on a tube. I had a blast. Bob, the rigger, drove the boat like a madman trying to knock me off. I held on for what seemed like forever. I was showing off, of course, but what the hell?

What the hell? I will tell you all about hell. I woke up the next morning in my hotel room and could not even walk to the toilet. For the next week both of my thighs were black and blue. In Memphis a few days later, the local crew had brought a bunch of jet skis to the river behind the Pyramid. Needless to say, I didn't join in the fun. That tour ended June 6. I flew back home to LA and had a little rest before I was back in the shop getting ready for another summer run on the Furthur Festival.

As always, I was out on the Dead for my birthday. This was the fifth year of this. We flew to Atlanta on June 21, 1998, and did production rehearsals June 22, 23, and 24 and started the tour at Lakewood Amphitheater on June 25. We did the normal summer run of sheds. We went from Lakewood to Blockbuster, Nissan Pavillion, Continental Airlines Arena, Nassua Coliseum, Great Woods, Entertainment Center in Camden, Saratoga Performing Arts Center, Darien Lake, Hartford Civic Center, Montage Mountain, Star Lake, Alpine Valley, Polaris, Pine Knob, Deer Creek, The World, Riverport, Fiddler's Green, Thomas and Mack, Irvine Meadows, and ended with two days at Shoreline Amphitheater, July 24 and 25.

This year, the Furthur run would be different for me. There was a girl on the tour that I had fancied for years. She was an amazing woman, strong, fearless, and amazingly nice. We spent almost every day off together running around in the cities that I had spent so many years exploring. She had never really toured before, so I showed her every place that I knew of. The two of us began to find that we really enjoyed many of the same things. I fell, and I fell hard. I would like to believe she did too, but I may never know how true that is. Anyway, for me it was awesome. Love was on the horizon, and it had been a pretty long time since I had felt that feeling.

LSD had a shop in Nashville, and I was headed there next. I got Deep Purple as my next gig. That turned out to be great. I went to the Nashville shop to prep the tour. I had never been to Nashville for any extended period of time. I was in the shop for a week, and it felt like forever. The weather was almost unbearable. I had forgotten how hot it got in the south. Growing up in Florida, you would have thought I would remember, but holy cow was I amazed.

We left Nashville to start the tour in NJ. The first show was on August 5 at the PNC Bank Arts Center. From there we went to Hartford, Boston, Long Island, Wilkes-Barre, Philly, Canandaigua, Detroit, Quebec City, Montreal, Toronto, Cuyahoga Falls, Chicago, Hinkley, Milwaukee, Denver, San Francisco, and Las Vegas, ending in LA on August 30. That tour was one of the best times I had ever had. It could have been the worst, though. We were staying at Holliday Inns most of the run. It was kind of low budget, but within a few days the whole crew found that we all got along great. Not to mention we all got to hear Deep Purple every night. The whole crew hung out every single day off. Whenever we would get to a city, we would all check in and take over the bar. We would spend the whole day drinking and goofing off. We went everywhere as a group. I really miss those days.

After that tour, I got to spend a bunch of time with my new "love," Killer. We went out to eat, saw movies, hiked all over LA and had a blast. Killer taught me that I did actually like sushi, and she introduced me to Thai food.

The beginning of relationships always amaze me. We had so much fun. She lived up in Topanga Canyon on the top of Greenleaf Canyon. To get to her place, you drove up a one-lane paved road for about two miles, then through a gate onto a dirt road for another mile or so. It was beautiful up there. We would spend hours sitting on the wraparound porch just talking about everything. Those were special times.

I left for another festival tour, the Family Values Tour, on September 21, 1998. I was sent out at the last minute to build a rig that was out over the audience. What should have turned into a great gig turned into another nightmare within a week. When I got out there, I found that the Icon system was a disaster. The guy that built it was pretty new, but the guys that were programming were not new at all. They had all been around forever, and they are still building and programming some of the biggest shows in the world. As far as I could tell, about a third of the rig was not working properly at all. Within an hour of arriving, I was up to my elbows in Icon parts, trying to help the Icon tech get out of the weeds. I worked all night and barely put a dent in the mess. When I finally got to the hotel, I fell in the bed and passed out.

When we got to the gig the next day, I started working on broken lights again. There was a show that night, the tour was starting, and I still had no idea what I was actually doing as far as my actual job. We did the show and loaded out, got on the bus, and woke up in Worcester, MA. That load-in was insane; there was so much lighting gear, set, and sound that every department was fighting with each other just to try and load in. I had never seen such a disaster. Somehow we got enough of everything working to do a show, and what a show it was. The line up was Orgy, Limp Bizkit, Ice Cube, Rammstien, and Korn. After the show, we loaded out, yelling at each other all the way until the last doors of the last truck were shut. The next day was a well-deserved day off in East Rutherford, NJ.

What I found out that day off was amazing. I met the crew chief, Cass, in the bar. I asked him what had happened during the prep, and he just shook his head and looked at the floor. This was his first tour for LSD, and the crew that he got was basically the bottom of the barrel. He said that none of the gear was in LA when they were putting it together. Everything was coming off other tours and straight out to them. Nothing was prepped and everything was broken. We basically built the whole rig from scratch during that first week on the road. I felt terrible for Cass. His Icon tech had no clue, his dimmer tech, Vid, had worked with me before on Furthur festival tours but was way over her head on this one. The two truss builders were as crazy as I was when I went on my first tour. And then there was Tony, the guy I did R. Kelly with a few years before, and myself.

Within a week, the Icon tech was sent home, and I moved into that spot. The dimmer person was replaced by Tack, "Turtle Boy" Tony took over my job building the FOH rig as well as setting up all of the consoles, and things started to work a little better. I was swamped with all of the broken Icons, as well as the new Icon wash lights. I would get up for load-in, get all of my lights sorted out as best as I could, set up a tech area, hang the lights, and fix as many lights as I could as we loaded in. Once the rig was up, I would work on lights again up until about an hour before doors and swap out as many broken lights as I could before the doors opened. That was my life for the whole tour. I don't think I ever had every light in the whole rig working for a whole show, but I sure did try.

One day during the show at the beginning of the tour, I got a call from Tony that a light was broken in the pit right in front of the stage. As was the case, I had never seen the show at all, due to the fact that all I had time for was fixing lights. (No big deal; it was my job.) Anyway I headed down into the pit and started to have a look at the light. Rammstein was on stage at the time, and it was terribly loud. I looked up at the stage just as the lead singer whipped around toward the front of the stage with this huge rubber cock in his hand. He points it at the crowd and starts yelling, and this milky white fluid comes shooting out all over me and the people behind me in the front row. I turned to work on the light just in time to see the whole lighting crew on the side of the stage laughing at me.

Jokes—yes, jokes—that is what always gets us through on the road. It never really matters how hard the job is or how long the day is, there is always enough time to take the piss out of each other. Some days we really are the fire hydrant. It's only fair, though. I have gotten to be the dog many times.

Speaking of being the dog, one day Joe, one of the truss builders, headed out into the crowd to find this little person. Tack has this phobia about little people, and everyone knew it, so Tony had seen this little person and called Joe to get a pass and get her on stage. Tack had to run motors during the show and could not leave his position at all during the show. Well, Joe found the little person, and talked her into stripping down to nothing and dancing for a whole song right in front of Tack. To see his face was unbelievable. We all just sat far enough away from him so that he could not take a swing at us and laughed.

That tour ran from NJ to Philly, Cleveland, Pittsburgh, Detroit, Milwaukee, Chicago, Minneapolis, Denver, Phoenix, LA, San Francisco, Las Vegas, Boise, Salt Lake City, Ft. Worth, Lafayette, New Orleans, Oklahoma City, Kansas City, St. Louis, Omaha, Kalamazoo, Indianapolis, Albany, and Uniondale, ending in Fairfax, VA, on October 31, 1998.

On November 1, the next day, we lost two of our six crew guys, drove to the Amphitheatre outside of Washington, D.C., and rebuilt the rig. From DC we hopped on the bus and headed to Toronto. On November 2 we played a smaller version of the tour at Arrow Hall. This new line up was Orgy, Incubus, and Korn. No one was really prepared for the tour to get extended, so, needless to say, none of us had any warm clothes. The answer to that was swag. Everyone on the crew all of a sudden looked like huge Korn fans. We all wore hoodies, sweatshirts, and caps with Korn logos. On that leg of the tour we left Toronto and headed to Montreal, Albany, Amherst, Lowell, Portland, Hampton, Charlotte, Lakeland, Miami, Atlanta, Knoxville, Houston, and Memphis, and then we ended on November 21 in Nashville.

That was the way the year ended for me. I flew back to LA and met up with my favorite girl. I spent the next week moving up the mountain. Killer and I had decided to live together. From the day that we started hanging out on tour until the summer that I moved to Vegas, we spoke every single day and found a way to see each other every three weeks. That was the way that we found how to make a relationship work for those that toured. It worked for us, and I bet it would work for everyone else if they could find a way. Three weeks is about as long as you can stay away from your partner while living on a bus. Things just get too crazy and you have to find a way to calm it all down.

1999
KORN/ZOMBIE, NICKELODEON, AMY GRANT

After spending a few months working around LA, I was back on the road. On February 21 I flew to Tucson and loaded in Korn/Rob Zombie. It was huge, just like the Family Values Tour. There were a lot of the same people out, but the lighting crew was different; I was the only person back out. This time around, we actually built the whole rig in the shop, and when we got to rehearsals we were in pretty good shape. Not that it would last for long, but at least we were starting out with working gear. We were in Tucson for four days of rehearsals, and then the first show. Within two days I was working my ass off again, fixing Icons.

Icons were pretty special lights. They would pretty much do whatever the programmer wanted them to do and they were really bright. The only problem with that is they break frequently when pushed to the limit. Korn and Rob Zombie needed to push the lights to the limit. That music just screams for it. Needless to say, I worked every day, non-stop. I was either fixing lights, loading in, or loading out. That had become a fixture of my life. I was the go-to guy for the big shows. I was not the only go-to guy, but I was one of the few that could keep a big rig working. The only problem was that the pay never got any better. By the time I was deep into this tour, that was really grinding at me. Touring was not so much fun anymore. I felt I was killing myself and never getting ahead. The drugs were still around, but they were not so much fun either.

That tour seemed to go on forever. From Tucson we went to Albuquerque, El Paso, San Antonio, Dallas, Biloxi, Jacksonville, Tampa, Miami, Dayton, Moline, Detroit, Hamilton, Toledo, Binghampton, Worcester, Providence, University Park, Philly, Chicago, Ft. Wayne, Grand Rapids, Greensboro, Greenville, Louisville, Birmingham, Little Rock, Madison, Fargo, Tacoma, Portland, Sacramento, Oakland, Bakersfield, and Anaheim, and it ended in San Diego on April 17.

There was a great story in Little Rock, where I got to be the dog again. The stage for this show was a huge turntable. On one side of the turntable was the Zombie set, on the other side was the Korn set. The guy that took care of the turntable was new. This was his first tour. When we were in Little Rock, after we had loaded in, we were all hanging out on the bus. Sure enough, here came the familiar knock. Someone opened the door and we all invited in Connie. As she made her way up the stairs, she looked straight at the new guy and said "I don't think we have met." I stood straight up and said "No, I know that you don't know him. Take him to the back and introduce yourself." Connie took him by the hand and he followed her like a puppy dog. I don't think he knew the stories of Connie, because when they emerged from the back he sat her down and put his arm around her. She just sat and smiled. The rest of the day, he introduced Connie to everyone as his new girlfriend. She was a true sport and played along. To this day, I'm not sure if anyone ever told him about Connie. I have to imagine he knows now, but you never know.

I was ready to die by the end of that tour. I was beat up and tired of not being paid what I thought I deserved. At least Killer and I were in great shape. That may have been the only thing that kept me going. She had a way of making it OK. She would make me forget how crappy it was out there. We spent May at home up on the mountain. She made the road, which I wanted to quit, bearable.

The first week of June, we began prepping the All That Music and More Festival. My old roommate, Kevin, and I were going to be the crew, and Killer was going to be a working lighting director. It was great in a lot of ways, because Kevin and I could keep the rig working no matter what, and Killer was my partner. It was bad in a whole lot of ways as well, because Killer and Kevin didn't like each other. As time has passed, I have had to apologize to both Kevin and Killer for my ways of dealing with several situations out there. It was hard on a lot of levels. But it was fun on so many more.

That tour started out with Kevin and I stuck at Chicago airport. A storm had come in and our flight was delayed landing. We missed the flight connecting to Indianapolis. Kevin and I had run through the airport just in time to see the plane backing away from the gate. We ended up staying in some hotel about fifteen minutes away.

The next morning we went back to the airport and caught the first flight out. Landed in Indianapolis, got a rental van, and headed out to (my favorite venue) Deer Creek for load-in. Killer had already started getting the lighting rig together, and Kevin and I were an hour late for work. Kevin had been on the road for several years longer than I had been, but between the two of us we could mark any lighting rig so that almost any-one on the planet could put it together without much supervision. Killer had all of the trusses laid out and bolted together and was starting to get the stagehands to run out the cable. Kevin and I were a bit surprised that so much work had been done. We were expecting to be in hell that day. There was a rehearsal that day and we thought for sure we would be way behind and everyone else on the crew would be yelling at us non-stop. Needless to say, Killer had done a great job all by herself. The day went along very well and everything was working just about on time.

We rehearsed in Indianapolis from June 12 to June 16. We had the first show on June 17. That tour ran through August 22. That was a great summer for Killer and I. All that time together was great. We did a run from the middle of the country through the Northeast, all the way down through to West Palm Beach, then across the southern states through to California, up that coast through Portland, then straight across the north-ern US all the way back to end the tour in Washington, D.C.

I was still doing a lot of blow. I don't think Killer ever had a clue that I was snorting blow the whole time we were touring together. When I think back, it is strange. I was always pretty good at keeping myself in line when I had to, so I guess I just found a way to do it when she was busy with other things. Funny thing is, the whole cocaine scene on tour was moving from out in the open to back rooms and secret friendships within tours. I guess that change in the scene was what helped me keep my use of coke far enough away from her that she just didn't know about it. At that point, there was always a small group of us that kept the drug very quiet and to ourselves.

There were days that seemed to never end. Those were the days when Killer and Kevin would refuse to even speak to each other. I was in love, so I had all kinds of issues to deal with at every turn. Kevin was in the right about three-quarters of the time, but there were times that I found myself on Killer's side when she was completely wrong. I wish the guy that crewed us all together would have taken a look at the situation a bit closer. By the time the tour was over, we all had found a way to deal with each other on some level, but from then until about 2008 there was animosity between Kevin and I. When we finally spoke about it after all of those years, I tried to take as much blame as I could. Kevin and I speak to each other online more often than we did in the past, and I am grateful for that.

Killer always went to bed early, and I would just hang with my blow friends till late in the evening getting high and then crashing in my bunk much later. For some reason, and I could not put my finger on it (other than maybe Killer knew I was still getting high), we started to drift apart. It was not anything major. Just a space started to exist that had not up until then. I didn't really pay much attention to it at that point. In hindsight, the Lord was starting to work his odd ways with me. I had drifted pretty far away from the church by then. I'm sure you can imagine how that could happen with the lifestyle that I was living. I was in no way ready to think through my spirituality. I was just in a funk of trying to make my life, career, and relationship work.

After that tour ended I was home for a few days, and then I went straight out on Sarah Brightman. That tour started in Reno. We worked our way south and had a day off in Santa Barbara. Killer was coming to see me, and I was really looking forward to seeing her. When she arrived at the hotel, we went to the room. I hopped on the bed with her, and then she calmly got up and sat in the chair. We proceeded to have a long chat about sex and relationships. The outcome of that conversation was that she wanted to lay off the sex and see if we actually could be as close without sex. WOW! To tell you the truth that was a shock to my system. I had no idea what to

176

think. I really didn't have much of a choice, so I decided that maybe she had a point and I would have to just follow her lead and see how things evolved. We went to dinner, then we went back to the room and slept. She left in the morning and I went to work.

The Sarah Brightman tour was awesome. I met one of my best friends out there, Stren. Stren was English in all ways. He had never wanted to go to the USA and hated every part of it until I took him to an American steakhouse. The steaks in England are expensive and not very good, so I proposed that we try the Metropolitan Grill in Seattle. He was hooked. All of a sudden he liked America a lot more than he ever though possible. In a magazine on one of the flights that we took on that tour, he found a list of the country's best steakhouses and showed me that we were playing almost every city on the list. So that became our mission. Well, that was one of our missions. The other, since almost the whole crew was English, was to try and snort all of the cocaine in the USA. We did a great job at both missions.

One of the coolest things for me on that tour was the venues that we played. Sarah Brightman had a fan base that went to opera houses, so the venues that we got to play were amazing. Of course there were some arena shows, but there were also some amazing theaters in towns that you would never imagine. In Portland we played the Arlene Schintzer Hall. That was far cry form the old Rose Garden.

We flew to Denver after Sacramento, and Stren had found that he wanted to eat at a place called Brook's Steakhouse. We checked into the hotel and made our way there. It was amazing. I could not sell him on the Buckhorn for buffalo, but after we loaded into to the Temple Buell Hall, another hidden theater treasure, I took him to the Rocky Mountain Diner for buffalo meatloaf. He was amazed! (The diner was forced to close in February of 2011, so there's no more of that great food.)

The next day we flew to Chicago, and yes, Stren had a place to eat. We ate at the Chop House. We also drank two bottles of Opus One. That was excellent. We played the Chicago Theatre the next day, and all of us did so much blow we could barely talk.

The next run we did was some more of those amazing theaters. We went to the Detroit Opera House, E.J. Performing Arts Center in Akron, The Benedum Center in Pittsburgh, The Aronoff Center for the Arts in Cincinnati, Shea's Theatre in Buffalo, Bushnell Auditorium in Hartford, the brand new Performing Arts Center in Newark, the Wang Center in Boston, Dar Constitution Hall in Washington, D.C., Kravitz Center in West Palm Beach, Ruth Eckerd Hall in Clearwater, and, the last on the list, and maybe my favorite (although it was very weird), the Jackie Gleason Theatre on Miami Beach.

I have stayed in touch with Stren through all of these years. He runs a huge rigging outfit in England. We don't talk nearly as much as we should, but he always has a home in the USA if he chooses to come! I flew back to LA from Miami and back up the mountain to see Killer. It was weird being there. The whole friend/no sex thing was really riding hard on my brain. I did and do love her, so I guess instead of listening to what the Lord was trying to express, I chose to go alone, or so I thought, and ride this horse through our changed relationship.

I did a bunch of one-offs in LA (from one day up to a week in the same venue). The next tour that was to come up was the Amy Grant Christmas tour. Killer was the lighting operator, I was the lighting crew chief, and I ended up with a whole crew of new young kids out of the Nashville LSD shop. Killer took me south from the mountain down the windy Pacific Coast Highway to LAX, where I hopped on a plane and went to Nashville to prep the tour.

Nashville in winter is heaven compared to the summer, when the shop is a nasty sweatbox. We put the show together and then loaded it into the rehearsal space in the Nashville hockey arena. It was fun getting a crew of young kids. They all really wanted to learn how to be good at what they did. Each one of them looked up to the guys that had been on the road. They all asked questions and paid attention when you would give them suggestions.

One of the crew was this beautiful young girl named June. When you looked at her you would have never thought that she was a roadie. She dressed nice, smelled nice, and always looked very presentable. You can imagine how quickly she got her stagehands to do anything she asked them to do. The best part about her was that she never once had any issues about strapping on a harness, climbing the circus ladder, and fixing a light in the rig. When the stagehands that were in love with her all day saw how hard she worked, they fell deeper and deeper in love. When it came to load-out every night, I would get the lighting hands and each one would ask to work with June.

I also had a girl doing dimmers for me. Viv was one of those strange people that you either hated or liked. Most of the stagehands around the country leaned toward the hate side. She was a decent-sized girl and could do dimmers for a medium-sized tour almost as well as any of the guys. The biggest problem that we all ran into was that she used to talk down to everyone around her. When I think back, I bet it was one of those survival techniques she used to show she could do the job as well as the guys. Whatever the case, she would cause headaches for me almost every day.

Viv and I did several tours after that, and I grew to like her. She really was good at putting rigs in and pulling them out. She was also really good at troubleshooting. I know the other crew chiefs would cringe when they were told Viv was on their crew, but I never minded. For some reason, when I would tell her to stop acting up, she just would. When I talked to some of my other friends that had her on their crews, they said they could never get her to stop. Whatever the reason, she was always great with me on the road. I think she is back in Chicago now working for the local.

June's Icon tech partner out there was a guy named Joe. He was young and very new. He would ask me how to do everything. For a while I would get frustrated, but as time went on he became so good that I found he had taught me more lessons than I would have ever imagined. By the end of the tour, our crew was amazing. I learned so many lessons from them—most of all about patience— that I can never repay any of them.

Killer showed up in Nashville a day before we loaded in the show for rehearsals. We went out to dinner and had a wonderful night. The next morning we went to the arena and loaded in all day. The lighting designer showed up later in the day, just when we had everything up and working, and started to have a look at the lighting system. She and Killer would stay up all night and program. I would hang out all night with them to fix anything that went down while they were working. I would take notes of the things that were up in the rig that needed to change, get fixed, or moved around. I would leave notes for the crew to work on the issues while I slept into the afternoon. To my surprise, they would almost have everything done by the time I came in.

Before the first night was over, the LD told Killer that one of the gobos that was in all of the Icons was wrong. It was a gobo that was made of broken pieces of diachronic colored glass. It projected a kaleidoscope effect on whatever surface it was projected on. The LD was adamant that the pro-jection of colors was too small and that we had put all of the wrong gobos in the lights. Before I go in too deep with this story, I have to give a little background on lighting designers.

First of all, there is a battle that has raged for ages. That battle has always been between the lighting and sound people that work on rock con-certs. Each of the people in charge of sound and lights will always be going at each other as to what is more important. The sound guys will always tell you that people come to the show to hear their favorite bands play live, and lighting guys will always say that the people come to *see* their favorite bands. It is a never- ending battle that always end with: "All you need is a great stereo system and you can hear your favorite band whenever you want. But if you do not light them up, what is the use in going to a show?"

To me, especially back then, it was an excellent marriage between sound and lights that gave me all of my memories. But as time progressed and technology pushed its way into the industry, the lighting side of things progressed much more quickly than sound. There were more digital toys in lighting before sound began to get all of their digital toys. Therefore, in the late '90s the world-wide famous lighting attitude of wanting everything all of the time and more toys than anyone can imagine was at a peak.

I have worked for so many different LDs. The funniest thing about most of them is the strange ego thing. Even the guys that came through the trenches as a tech seem to forget that they once did the things that they are now asking for. They once stood on the other side of the ranting that they are now dishing out. Being a tech as long as I was, I learned that some things just will not change. Everyone wants the impossible, and my job will always be making the impossible happen. I finally learned that the impossible is not always impossible!

After getting the news that we had put the wrong gobos in all of the lights, which was a total of about fifty lights, I called the shop and told them the news. What I got as an answer was: "That is not true. Fran [the lighting designer] had designed those gobos a year before and she was the only one using them. They were put in storage last year and had just been taken back out for her and this tour." Well, I went out to where they were working and tried to explain to Fran what I was told. (Probably not the best solution.) I proceeded to get quite an earful about how I had no idea what

I was talking about and that I had better find a way to get the right gobos out here before we left rehearsals.

I must thank June and Joe for getting up in that rig and swapping every gobo out. By the time they had climbed around the whole rig and swapped them all, it was time to load out. Not once did they complain about having to do the work, even knowing that when they were finally done, the LD would never even have time to see the results. That was the day that I figured it out that I was going to have a stellar crew by the end of the run.

LA-based tours and Nashville-based tours are two separate monsters, mostly in terms of the status of the different crew leaders and members. On the Nashville-based tours you're more likely to find that the people with the higher-up jobs have bigger attitudes. This just happened to be one of those tours. The tour manager on this one seemed to have had a problem in the past with yelling at and hitting people that worked for him.

We had an altercation in Raleigh, NC. At some point before the show, I had to run from FOH to backstage to get a jacket for Killer. I held up my pass to the house security guy as I passed, and he yelled at me to stop. Well, the show was about to begin, so I told him I would be right back and he could look at my pass closer. Well, at some point right about the same time, there was a sound guy that looked like me who was working on part of the PA right next to the same security guy. The sound guy was so tired of listening to the house security guy that he just ignored him every time he was asked to show his pass.

When I passed by the house security guy on my way back, he was having a heated conversation with our tour manager. The house guy pointed at me and said, "That's him!" I had no idea about the sound guy's antics until about halfway through the earful that I was getting. The orchestra for the band was standing right there, so I said we should probably go somewhere else so that he would not get in trouble for doing something extreme. As we walked down the backstage hall, I tried to explain that it was not me and that the house security guy had the wrong guy. As I got the last words out of my mouth, he opened the door to where the video guys were working and laid into me about how I was lying and there was no reason for the house guy to lie to him. When he finished his yelling, I took my pass off from around my neck and handed it to him, explaining that I worked for him and if he was choosing the word of someone he had never met before over the word of his lighting crew chief, he could find another. I was going home.

I walked past him out to the bus, packed my bags, and headed back to the production office to see if I could get a ride to the airport. As I entered the office, the tour manager was on the phone with my boss from the lighting company. I have no idea what was said, and to tell you the truth I didn't really care. The tour manager hung up the phone, and the production manager and I sat in the office alone. He told me I should just apologize and get on with things. Well, I had had enough of all of that, and I was not about to apologize and let him off the hook just because of his title. As I was trying to get a cab to take me to the airport, the tour manager walked in and asked the production manager to leave.

There I was, face to face again with him. He reached out to grab my hand, but instead handed me my pass and said he was sorry. He'd identified the sound I'd said was really to blame. He had gotten it wrong. I felt kind of cool about that, but I have always kept my ears and eyes open when I ended up on any Nashville tours.

That was probably the most exciting thing that happened on that tour. Killer and I seemed to be getting along well. Right around then was when she started to tell me how I needed to start looking into becoming a production manager. She started coming up with all of these reasons that I would make a good one. I was pretty happy doing what I was doing. I was, however, hoping to be making better money by this point, and it didn't seem like that would happen in the near future. As a matter of fact, when that tour ended and I was back in LA, the same things started happening that had always happened in the past.

I ended up on a millennium show. It was the Bee Gees, in Ft. Lauderdale. I was sent out as just an Icon tech and someone else was the crew chief, yet they had no clue as to how to build the system. After I got there, I was thrown right back into the familiar place of saving the day. I was never paid like a crew chief, but I was definitely expected to step up and do someone else's job if the work needed to be done.

I was about to explode at that point. There He was again, asking me to change. Jesus was finding his way into my life at the strangest places. At the time I was just mad and frustrated, but that comes with the lessons that I am always being taught.

Not long after Killer and I had gotten back to LA, she brought up the idea about me being a production manager again. I was pretty sure I had no chance of even getting a foot in the door of that career, so I usually just blandly entertained the thought until she stopped talking about it. That worked pretty well for a good while.

I was doing a lot of one-offs all over LA then and didn't really have a tour lined up anytime in the near future. Then, all of a sudden, one would pop up and off I would go around the country again.

ED AND TED'S

One Sunday, I was sitting around the mountain place and I got a phone call from this guy Ted. He ran a small lighting company south of LA down in Vista. A lot of the guys that I had worked closely with at LSD had been doing shows for them now and again, but I had never really ventured away from LSD much. I was pretty surprised when all of a sudden I was speaking with Ted. It was actually a very funny conversation. We literally just talked about life in general for about forty-five minutes. After that he brought up the fact that he needed a crew chief for the Red Hot Chili Peppers. He offered me five hundred dollars a week more than LSD was paying me, and promised to keep me working on tours for him after that one ended. He said that he had some decent-sized clients, and he needed someone to come in and build his crews.

I was shocked, to say the least. For the first time in my life, I was actually wanted for something other than just to fix shows that were in some kind of mess.

The Chili Peppers was a good long run. It was ten legs, each three and a half weeks long, with ten days off in between each leg. I was going to make full salary on the road and half salary as a retainer for the time off in between legs. There was no way that I was going to turn that down. I was really worried that I would burn the bridges that I had built with LSD, but the pay was good, and Ted seemed like a great guy. I made Ted promise to put me on more shows when that tour ended, and I took the job.

My friend RJ had told Ted about me. He had left LSD a few years before that and gone to run Ed and Ted's shop. So it turned out I owed the next four years of my career to RJ. He pulled me out of the hole that I was in and set in motion what was going to be a long and great relationship with Ed and Ted. We did amazing shows together. By the time that had run its course, RJ's introduction had catapulted me into the production manager role that Killer was so happy to bring up all of the time.

The Chili Pepper tour was a bit of a mess, but it was new for me, and I really wanted to succeed, so I just bulled my way through it. We did more cocaine than you could imagine! I swear, every day we had more. It was cocaine and golf, actually. In the middle of all of that, we did shows. It was pretty cool.

The Chili Peppers would only do two nights in a row, and then they had to have a day off. So there were four of us that started playing golf on the days off. Two sound guys, the rigger, and me. We were allowed to give away as many tickets as we wanted, so before long the production assistant was just handing us memos with the address and name of some exclusive golf club that we would be playing at. I have no idea how many tickets she gave away for us to play golf, but some of the places that we played were amazing. By the end of the tour I was shooting in the eighties, which is amazing to anyone who has ever seen me play golf!

As you can tell, there are thousands of stories that each tour holds. Each tour just adds to the long story. The places that you go and the people that you meet become a huge family of stories within stories. By this time I was no longer interested in the cities that I visited. I just got up on a bus each morning and did my job. The fun was still there and the people that I shared time with were great, but the monotony of the travel all bundles up into itself.

While working at Ed and Ted's (2000 through 2004), I did lots of new bands and new types of venues. I worked for The Foo Fighters, Blink 182, Jane's Addiction, Mary J. Blige, Jack Johnson, The Goo Goo Dolls, Lollapalooza, and The Brian Setzer Orchestra. I did several legs for each of these bands. I actually got to Europe when I worked for Mary J. Blige. That was a trip, and quite the learning experience.

I was still doing blow, drinking tons, and enjoying my road life. I thought I didn't need the Lord in my life. I had everything going exactly the way that I had chosen things to be. I never really left my spiritual self, I just chose not to pay attention to the Lord. I was running things my way, and I knew what I needed in my life.

Somewhere in the middle of my new life at Ed and Ted's, Killer and I started to drift pretty far away from each other. I was in no way ready for that to end, and I really tried to change a lot about myself just to keep things together. But that was not ever going to be the way. I didn't know it at the time, but I was in for a huge learning experience.

I did love Killer, more than anything. I seriously believed that we would work through the weird road life and all that comes with it. I was wrong, and, as the story unfolded, the Lord was working his way back into my life. I was not ready for Him, and I really didn't have any idea that it was happening, but He was picking me up and carrying me to the next step of my life.

It was the beginning of the summer in 2002, and Killer and I were home together for a week or so before she was leaving on another tour. We argued and ignored each other most of the week. It was a terrible week, and I had no idea that we were headed straight into a brick wall. We were, though, and the day before she left, we sat down and talked.

We talked about what we saw for the future. After about two hours of serious discussion, we came to several completely opposite opinions about our lives together. We never really fought over all of the years that we spent together, and this wasn't really a fight either. We just let everything out, and came to a complete understanding that we both wanted and expected different things from each other. I know I cried most of that night, and when I dropped her at the airport we were both crying. We knew it was almost over. We knew deep down that we would not be able to fix the issues that existed. We also knew that all of the work that we had put into the relationship was over.

I left on tour a week later. We spoke a few times on the phone while she was programming for her tour, but it was not like before, when we made time for each other every day. I cried that week so many times. I was a mess, and I knew I was in for a ride.

Eventually, we quit speaking at all. I'm pretty sure I started that by not answering the phone for a couple of days. I was so devastated. I thought I would die. In a way, I did. It was the first step toward me finding my way back to the Lord. I didn't know it, and would not come to that conclusion for many years, but that was the summer of my awakening. I would fight the Lord for ten more years, but He just held me tight and showed me His Grace.

I had made up my mind that if I didn't hear from Killer when I got back home from that tour, I was leaving. I got home and sat in that house for a week, Then I packed all of my things and moved to Vegas.

Right around this time, Ed and Ted's was evolving into a new entity. There were new faces around, and the old ones were starting to disappear. The company was getting big, and the small family vibe that all roadies search for was going away. I thought I was going to weather that storm, but before long I had dug another grave there. I was still touring for them, but I didn't feel very comfortable.

Vegas turned into one of the biggest messes I could ever imagine. I showed up there broken-hearted and could have cared less what my life would become. I gambled every night and drank more than I ever had in my whole life. It was fun for a good while, and then reality set in. I had gotten to the point that I was drinking a case of beer a day, and a bottle of Jack Daniels every two days. I was also finding a way to get to the black-jack table every evening. I stayed there drinking and gambling for eight months.

One morning I woke up, and knew I was going to die. I was killing myself, and I had no hope for survival in that city. I had no real friends there, and I had completely begun to destroy my body and mind. I sat on the bed that morning, as sick as I have ever been in my life, and cried deeply. By the time I pulled it together, I knew that I had to get back to Tampa. I needed my family. That would be my only hope for survival. I knew deep down inside I had destroyed everything in my spiritual and physical life. I was at the end, and something made me care.

I packed all of my things into a trailer and headed back to Tampa. I was depressed, scared, and very lonely. I had no idea what I would do when I got to Tampa, I just knew that I had to be there.

My mom hugged me when I walked in the door. Funny how good that makes you feel, no matter how old you get. She had a friend that lived in some condos down in South Tampa who had told my mom that there were a few for sale. I bought one. I went out on tour just after I signed all of the papers and made the down payment. I spent the summer with Lollapolooza. When the tour ended, I went back to Tampa to start making a home for myself.

I was home for a few months, and then I headed out to do the Brian Setzer Orchestra's Christmas Extravaganza. That ran through the beginning of the year. That would be the last tour I did for Ed and Ted's, as well as the last tour that I was a lighting guy, for the time being. I was seriously butting heads with one of the new salesmen, and I guess I had just had enough. We drew a line in the sand, and I ran across it faster than a cheetah. I broke the rules and got myself dismissed from my position there.

Being without a job, I had to figure something out. I was supposed to do Blink 182 again for Ed and Ted's, but that was out. I called the production manager, and he offered me the carpenter job. I took it, and became a carpenter instead of a lighting guy. Well, that was another big wasp nest that I walked into.

The stage manager and I didn't get along at all. We argued every day. It didn't help that he and the production manager were good friends. With about two weeks left in the tour, in Boston, at Great Woods, he jumped on me in the loading dock. He was twice my size, and I got pummeled. By the time the two weeks had past, I knew I was done there as well. I had no idea where to turn next. I thought every door was shutting, but in reality, the Lord was sending me exactly where I needed to be.

The pinnacle of my experience would be working with Brian Setzer. At the time that I went out on that tour, I had no idea what was in store for me. My whole world would get shaken up, and Mr. Setzer was about to let me into his world. I was in for a ride that I never could have imagined.

I was driving down the road, and my phone rang. The tour manager for Brian Setzer, Harry, was on the line, and out of the blue he asked me if I wanted to be the stage manager/carpenter for the upcoming tour. I said yes. What I found out was the lighting designer, Joe, who I got along with great, knew I had gotten fired from Ed and Ted's and had recommended me for this job. Little did I know, but that would be one of the best things that happened to me in my life.

I went out on the tour and found that I was pretty good at the job. We did a run through the States, and everyone involved out there started to gel together. We all began looking out for each other and really enjoying the time that we spent on the road. It had been such a long time since I'd had that feeling. It was like walking into a brand new LSD again. I was getting paid more than I had ever been paid, and Mr. Setzer toured a lot, so I stayed pretty busy most of the year.

It was fine that I lived in Tampa because the tour manager lived in LA, where all of the gear was stored, and he dealt with most of the everyday needs there. He would fly me out before tours so we could get everything together properly, but for the most part he took care of it. About the same time, I had run into some guys that I worked with years before in Tampa. They were doing a lot of work in Orlando and asked me to work with them. So when I was home I did shows with them, as part of the union.

Everything was starting to calm down. I was beginning to feel pretty good about my life again. Somehow, the Lord always knows the lessons that you need to learn. He always keeps you in His arms and sends you off to make yourself whole. I wish I had realized that at the time, but to me, I just felt calmness. I was near my family, working regularly, and paying my bills.

The next year, we did a tour in the States, Europe, and Japan. I had a blast on all of those tours. I saw the world in a whole new way. I was not frustrated in my job. I liked it again! On days off, we would all go see the cities we were in and enjoy the days together. When we were in Japan, though, I got a whole new bomb dropped on me.

Harry came to me one day, in the office, and said, "Tag, you're it. You are now the production manager." Well, I was a friend of the current production manager, Bill. I didn't want to make him mad, and I really had no idea how to do that job. Harry said it was all sorted out. Bill would be paid the same just to do the guitars, and I would be the stage and production manager. I told him I really didn't want the job, but he refused to have it any other way. He told me he would teach me and I would be fine.

When we got back to the States, I had three weeks to get the Christmas tour together. Harry was a dream. He literally walked me through every step of the job. We worked on all of the emails together, and he showed me the ropes well. I know I messed up several times on the first tour, but he was great at getting me back on track and fixing whatever I messed up. Harry taught me just about everything I would need to learn in that position. He took his time and gradually had me doing almost all of the things that he used to take care of in the beginning. He had a great way of just dumping a job on me and letting me figure it out. He also had me go through the hard processes of getting an answer from upper management.

Everything that gets done has to go through upper management, and usually they have never toured before and have little knowledge as to how anything works on the road. Deadlines and people's time are irrelevant when they get involved. I know it sounds kind of harsh, but in reality it is not. Upper management just wants to get the job done right. Sometimes it is a bit trying, but in the end the process is worth the effort.

For example, one day Harry called me and told me we needed to build a touring Stray Cats sign. It needed to be the size of a backdrop and it needed to have lights in it. And we needed it in a month and a half. He gave me a few ideas and a few contacts and told me to get it taken care of. Well, no one had a picture of what they wanted, and no one could even tell me what they thought that they wanted. I got on the phone and talked with a set company out in LA, and they kind of laughed as I asked them to come up with some ideas. Anyway, they did start working on it, and within a few days I had two drawings. One was of the "Cat Head," and another was a rendition of a guitar on an album cover. They looked great, so I sent them to Harry for approval. He came back and said that that was not what they were looking for, and that I needed to get more drawings. So I did. That went on for several weeks.

We were running out of time to get the sign actually built, and I still didn't have any answers on what we should build. Finally, at the last possible moment, I got a picture of show poster that someone at management had seen. Management said they wanted that. So I sorted through all of the issues with getting the project done. It was literally delivered to a sound stage in Chicago one day before we left the studio to start on tour. Talk about waiting till the last second. That happens a lot, but I had no idea, until Harry put me in the spot to learn. As I said, the end result is always worth the effort that everyone puts into it. All of the changing of minds produces some amazing work, even if it's at the last minute. Harry was a great teacher. I owe him.

As time passed, I started to find that spending time on the road with one band was pretty cool. I would see the same people every time we did a show or a tour. We all started to become really close. The crew that we have now has been together for about five years. We all look out for each other and keep in touch when we are not together on the road. Of course, there are times when we have a single show somewhere and we need a replacement for one or two of the guys, but for the most part we all try to stay as open with our schedule as we can. The only conclusion that I have come to is that we all have learned to care about and respect Brian Setzer.

Brian Setzer is probably one of the best guitar players in the world, definitely the best rockabilly player ever to walk the planet. As we have traveled around this planet, you can't even imagine the people that we have run into who have shown up and given him respect. Once, when we were in Vegas shooting a Monday Night Football commercial, Richie Sambora and Mr. Setzer joked about the "girl" guitars that come from New Jersey, as compared to the "manly" guitars from Long Island. At one point Richie would not even come out of his dressing room the jousting got so funny. That shoot was awesome. Brian was the musical director, and he had all kinds of people playing on that stage.

We were in Europe one summer, and we did a festival in Belgium. The Doors (Robby Krieger and Ray Manzerek) played before Brian played. When they came off the stage and back to the dressing room complex, they bypassed their own dressing rooms and went straight to Brian's. I'm not sure it was the best time, as he was getting ready to go on stage, but (WOW) it was The Doors. As soon as Brian went onstage, Robbie Krieger sat down in a chair on the side of the stage and looked like a child, eyes as big as the sun, watching Brian play. I was amazed. He stayed right there until his manager came to get him when his ride was leaving.

Another time I was showing him the way to the stage from the bus, just before the show, and we walked right into Paul Stanley. Brian stopped everything and spoke with him for about five minutes before he went on stage. That is one of the things that you learn quickly. Brian is a very thoughtful and respectful gentleman. When you think about the old times in America, when people really took the time to notice and acknowledge each other, Brian is in that category. Rock star or not, he is a gentleman first, and everyone who works with him knows that. We all respect that and have learned to act that way as well. He treats each of us very well and does an amazing job to make sure that we are as comfortable as possible out on the road.

The respect that is generated within our little group is amazing. It surrounds every aspect of our touring, from the first email I send out to each venue to the last phone call that I make before we show up at a venue. Yes, there are certain things that we must have in order to do the show, but the idea of demanding things never crosses my mind. We need to treat each other with respect, we are all here together, and we are not going anywhere. The show will happen, and we will all have to work together to make that happen.

I am positive that the Lord put me in this situation to learn that lesson. In the last nine years, I have learned to re-read every email that I have sent out to make sure that I am respectful and caring. Firm sometimes, yes, but respectful. I have learned to bite my tongue on many occasions instead of losing my mind. In some form or fashion, through the time that I have spent out with this tour I have found an inner peace. I am thankful that I have been able to experience the stressful situations and the problems. They have led me to look for solutions in many aspects of my life.

When Harry left the tour, I think the first thought in everyone's mind was "What do we do now?" He was the leader. He was like a huge ball of sticky gum that everything stuck to. He had all of the info, and all of a sudden he was gone. He called me to tell me he was moving on to something else, and during that call he listened to all of my concerns and worries, giving me back the knowledge that I needed to just step up and keep things moving in the direction that he'd been leading us. He told me I knew everything I needed to know and I would be just fine. He also gave me an open line to call him when I needed info or a little help. I did call him. In fact, I think I wore out my welcome in about two years of phone calls. He sure was helpful for that time. We see each other several times a year now, but we never speak for long about work.

When I have thought about the time that Harry was a part of my life on tour, I thank the Lord that I had a chance to have a father figure for one part of my adult life. Losing my dad when I was twenty-one was a real shocker. I pretty much ran from everything that I knew. I have spent almost all of the time from that point on trying to figure out whom to please. When I have conversations with other men who lost their fathers when they were young, we all have the same problem. We are left with a huge hole in front of us. That hole is the whole concept of growing up.

In America, we learn when we are kids that we must do better than our parents did. We take that thought and somehow think that we are supposed to impress our fathers with our accomplishments in life. To a certain extent, I believe this to be true, so when you lose your father, all of a sudden there is no one to impress. All of a sudden you are sent out on a journey to find someone to impress.

I have a lot of people that I call friends in LA. Each one of them played important roles in my understanding of life. There have been several father figures throughout that time of my life. I thank each and every one of them in a prayer.

As time passed, out on the tours without Harry, I found new ways of getting things done and explored ways that have become "my way." As I said earlier, we are a small family out there now. I don't know how long it will stay that way, but for now it is perfect, and everything has progressed exactly the way that it should.

THE UNDERSTANDING

Harry has been gone from this tour for several years now. Things have changed. Brian has built new bands and the world is a little different now. I realized that I needed to be in LA to do what I do for a living. I also knew that with the economy going south, it was getting very hard to ask management to fly me out and get hotels and rental cars every time work needed to be done. I also came to the conclusion that it was not fair to Brian Setzer. I wanted to keep doing this tour, and I was asking a lot of him to let me live in Florida and work in LA. So, as things happen, everything started to fall in place for me to be able to pack up and move back out to LA.

My finances had built themselves back up, so I just needed to find a place to live. It just so happened that we were going to Australia in March, so I would have to get the gear in a sea container just about the same time I needed to find a place out in LA. I went to LA to load the container, and I used my time out there to have a look at a place a friend had told me about. It was perfect: just outside of downtown, on a mountain, and the owner lived on the property. We spoke for a long time about the apartment. He showed me everything, but it was unnecessary. I had fallen in love with it as soon as I drove up the street. I flew home the next day and started to formulate a plan to get my things out to LA.

I had some time off before we went to Australia, so I decided to pack a truck, drive my stuff to LA, and store it until I could get out there and move in. I was actually pretty nervous and scared about packing up again and moving across the country. I was having a terrible time making decisions about what to take and what to throw away. I had been in my condo for eight years and had acquired a lot of things. I had never planned on moving back to LA, but I knew I had to. So I overcame my hesitation, got the truck, packed it up, and headed off.

The truck only had a stereo, no CD player or anything, so I was at the mercy of the radio for the next few days. The first day, I listened to whatever stations would come in. I like classic rock mostly, so I searched for that all day long. I made it to Alexandria, Louisiana, that day. I stayed in a hotel, showered, and took off in the morning. The radio was pretty bad that day, so I found a talk show and started to listen to that. It turned out to be a Christian station, and it was very interesting. The program was about packing things up and making a new life. As I sat there listening and driving, I almost felt as if someone had gotten in the truck with me and started talking about my life. This went on all day. Program after program practically charted the chronological order of my life, beginning with my first trip out to LA, twenty years before.

The radio became my whole world. The topics of every program were so relevant to my life. I was in another world. It was as confusing as it was interesting. I mean, how was this happening?

I stopped in Dallas and saw an old friend from high school for a few days. I stayed for 2 days. We drank the whole time I was there. I was thinking that this was what my life had become. I was going to be "that guy" that whenever you see, you drink. It was as if high school had never ended.

From there I headed toward Las Vegas. I was going to spend a few days with one of my favorite friends in the whole world, Eve. She and I had been through the trenches together. We have always stayed in touch and always made sure each other was OK. The times that I have spent with her are times I would never trade for anything on this planet.

My plan was to stop in Albuquerque, but when I got there I wasn't tired. That whole day in the car, I kept thinking about what my life had been and what I was getting myself into now. I was thinking about all of the people I had tried to please through the years. I was thinking losing my Father in my life so early and trying to replace that void with people that I had met. As much as the Setzer camp was like a family, when Harry left, a huge void was left there, as well. This void had followed me through all of the relationships. I always seemed to give everything of myself to someone else, or I thought that I was. I was starting to understand that I needed to turn inside of myself and contemplate who, or what I wanted to please. As I listened to the radio, I began to realize that God was with me, and that I needed to begin to pay attention to myself. The fact that I needed to surrender to God, and let him take control of my life hit me like a brick.

I kept driving. I ended up stopping in Gallup, NM. I pulled off of the freeway and drove up the main drag looking for a place to stay. I passed a bar that looked open, and then I drove straight up to the El Ranch Hotel. Wow, was that place cool-looking. It was straight out of the '50s. I pulled in and got a room. After driving all day, I just wanted a beer, a shot, and some sleep. The bar at the hotel was closed, so I brought my stuff up to the room, grabbed a bit of money, and headed out in the cold to that bar that I had passed.

It was freezing cold outside. All I had was a sweatshirt and jeans, so I pulled up my hood and started walking. There was not a soul on the street. It was pretty weird. I walked up to the door of the bar, opened the door, and walked in. As I pulled off my hoody and took a look around, everyone was staring at me. It seemed I was the only white person in the bar. All at once, the whole world started to make sense. All of a sudden, I knew deep down inside that I was going to learn the biggest lesson of my life. All of time that I had spent studying Native American religion didn't matter anymore.

I have never been prejudiced in my life. I have never really found a place for that in my world, but at that moment, I knew I was a minority. I also had no idea how to proceed. My first thought was to just turn around and leave, but then I changed my mind and just walked straight up to the bar and ordered a beer and a shot. I drank the shot, turned, saw a table next to the door, walked over, and sat down to finish the beer. It seemed as though all eyes were staring at me. I am not sure that was the case, but as I was drinking that beer, I started to become very nervous. I was just about done and ready to get up and leave when the bartender came by and asked if I wanted another. I felt like I was stuck in one of those never ending dream cycles that the *Twighlight Zone* was so good at portraying. I didn't know what to do. I said yes and figured I would come up with some way of leaving quietly while I drank that beer.

When the beer came, two guys sat down at the table with me and we started talking. They asked all kinds of questions. I really knew I should not have been answering them, but what could I do? Before long, they started asking about a ride home. I told them I walked, and then they just laughed and asked, "From Dallas?" I was caught. One of the guys disappeared before long, and I was sitting with one guy, begging me to drive him home so he didn't have to walk in the cold. I could not find a way out. I searched my mental files the whole time that we talked to figure out some way to get out of that bar, walk the two blocks back to the hotel in the cold, and be safe. I came up with nothing. I guess that nervous energy that was building earlier had a reason.

I was sitting there thinking about what I would do if all of a sudden the rental truck, everything that I own, and my identification got taken in Gallup, NM. What in the world had I led myself into this time? The only option I could think of was to be respectful and friendly. I made myself say yes and hoped for the best.

As we got up to leave the bar, this big guy came out the door with us. He started giving me a hard time, and I just kept answering him politely. He walked with us for a block and then went in some building. We kept walking, and finally the guy that I was going to drive into my demise looked back and told me the other guy was not following us. When we got to the hotel parking lot, I walked up to the rental truck and said, "This is everything that I own. I'm gonna drive you wherever you want, but please know I am thinking the worst." He didn't answer. He just got in.

As I was getting in, I may have been more scared than I have ever been in my life. We rode without saying anything until we were about a block from where we would turn off. As we sat at a light, he said something about being depressed. I looked at him and said, "Yeah, we all get depressed. You look like you're about my age, and this is a really hard time for me, too." I told him that my job was not as much fun anymore after losing Harry as my mentor. I had no idea why I had worked my whole life just so that everything I owned would fit in this truck. Why was I moving three thousand miles from my family to start something, to make my life real? We turned into a trailer park and just kept talking. It was amazing that we had just started talking about all of the things that I was listening to on the radio for the last two thousand miles.

He told me to pull over and let him out, and I noticed a car with the lights on at the end of the street. That is when I really thought I was done for. But we just kept talking. The car with the lights on pulled away after about five minutes. We talked for another ten minutes or so, and then he said he had to go inside and get some sleep. As he started to open the door, he stopped. He turned back around and said, "You were right. My cousin and I were going to take this. But as we were talking, I realized that we were the same, that people are all the same, we just come from different worlds." He got out of the truck and thanked me for talking with him. The last thing he said before he walked away was, "Imagine that, and with a white guy."

I was shaking in my clothes as I started to drive. I didn't know if it was over or just about to begin. I made it back to the hotel, parked the truck, and went to my room. I passed out, got up in the morning, showered, and got out of there. I think I drove about five hundred miles before all of that really sunk into me. What in the world was I thinking? Apparently I was not thinking, and I had not been thinking for years. I had been putting myself in the line of fire my whole life. Somehow, the Lord knew how to get me to accept him into my life, for real.

Later that day, as I was heading toward the Hoover Dam, I was listening to a guy talk about Revelations. I listened to him preach his knowledge that the end of the world is near. I swear, I was watching the road, and Jesus was asking me to have him in my life. I can't explain it any more than that. My world, the one that I had been living, was at an end. There was no question about that. What was in store for the future was anyone's guess. I was safe and in His arms again. He had made sure of that!

JUDGMENT

With all that had just occurred in that time, my mind churned with the need to use the understanding that I had been given. I yearned for more conversations with God. I still do to this day. I can't wait to hear what others have to say to me. Somehow, God has found his way to show me more than I could have ever imagined. He speaks to me all day, every day. I have found a solace that I never knew could exist in my life. I find myself smiling for most of the day. It is amazing, as I pass by other people the smile seems to spread to others. I have found myself in great conversations with strangers, whereas I used to be pretty shy about opening up. Since that time in the desert, I have begun to see things a little differently. Everyone does seem to be the same, we all have just found a different way to get to that point.

That brings me to the simple thought of judgment. As with all of us, I have found that I spent most of my life judging everything that passed by me. From my earliest memories, I have judged people and things. All of that judgment had gotten me nowhere. I had spent most of my life making decisions based on a judgment of some kind. So many people had gotten the short end of my thoughts due to my ignorance. All of the time spent on the road without a single smile has worn through my skin.

The shows seemed so important, yet the most important things were the people I knew and experiences we shared. I thank the Lord for opening my eyes. I thank the Lord for giving me the strength to get on with his life for me. I thank the Lord for taking me on his back as I stumbled through the life that I had led. We are all able to use the free will that the Lord gave us through Adam and Eve. We are all capable of producing an argument based on our thoughts and ideas, yet I have found that the biggest argument we must begin with is the argument based on how we answer to our maker.

The most astounding lesson that I have learned is that I need Jesus in my life. I have found with that first step, that first realization that I had no control of my life, that the life I lead is not mine at all. This life is our Lord's life. I have found and will keep on finding myself on the edge of judgment. I am a sinner, and I am a fool, but in my foolish ways, I have promised myself to learn.

I still find myself making quick judgments about a person or an idea. But I am catching myself sooner and sooner after making that judgment. I hope, as time progresses, I find a way to dismiss that judgment from the start.

As I sat, as a stranger, in a church once, I heard a lesson given to us by our Lord. It is the parable from the book of Mark, Chapter Four, verses twenty-six through thirty-four. It is a parable of planting a seed.

Jesus spoke of God's kingdom. He explained that God's kingdom is like a seed that is thrown on the earth and forgotten about. The seed sprouts and grows in its own time and manner. The earth does it all without the help of any man. Before long, the plant is fully ripened and is then available for harvest. It speaks of how the simplest, smallest seed will erupt into a huge tree, a tree full of life that will provide shelter to birds. Jesus provided this message to his disciples in a story to show them the ways of his Father.

We are all planted here on this earthly kingdom to grow and ripen. As we mature through our experiences on this planet, we have the opportunity to make our way to harvest. Once we are harvested, we may spread the experience with those around us. God really does have a plan for each and every one of us. We may not have any idea what that plan is as we begin to grow, but when we start to be harvested by our Lord, we begin to understand. God begins to give us the answers we have been seeking all along. He gives us the chance to look at the paths that we have chosen in order to find our way to those branches.

The lessons that I have learned on my path may not be anything like the lessons you have learned. My trials and tribulations through sex, drugs, and rock and roll were what I needed to form the sprouts which will hopefully allow me to be harvested for the Lord. I look forward to the lessons ahead which will, hopefully, allow me to sort through the tangles and knots that I have created.

As I look back, I am not proud of many of the choices that I made on my journey. But as with all of us, I made them and I must live with them. I have asked forgiveness from those that I have hurt or judged along my path, and I will keep doing so. I have chosen to pay attention to my daily life, my thoughts and actions, and the very minutes of my day. It is actually quite refreshing to make sure that I am smiling throughout the day. The smiling leads to good thoughts and good deeds. But the best thing that I have personally found through smiling is that I thank God for saving me many more times during my day.

The Grace of God is unimaginable. He watches over you and allows you to grow and learn on your own playing field. When everything is going to pieces in your life, he gives you the option of letting him handle it. I know from experience that the hurt of letting him have control can be rough, but as soon as you let him take control, he makes everything happen exactly the way that it should happen. The path may be scary, but when you join him on that walk, the smiles and the peace are worth all of the pain that you have caused yourself. He is the answer for me, and he may be the answer for you. Give yourself the freedom to choose without judgment, and see where that path leads you! You may be as surprised as I am.

Several years ago, I heard a voice in my head tell me to write. It just said that I should write. I started writing about all of the things that I had done in my life. I wrote about all of the places I had been. I wrote about this giant party that you have just read about. I thought that is what this book was going to be about. I thought that all of the sex, cocaine, and acid were the things that I wanted to share with you. I thought that I should be the one to let the cat out of the bag about "life on the road of rock".

What I found was that I needed to find myself. I needed to write and share my thoughts and dreams. I needed to take a good look at my life, my ways, and me. Through that process, I found a way to be a storyteller. Maybe the storyteller can help you get to your final destination.

Thanks for your time!

By the way….. I'll have the Mute!